THE

LOUISIANA

NATIVE

GUARDS

THE LOUISIANA NATIVE GUARDS

THE BLACK MILITARY EXPERIENCE DURING THE CIVIL WAR

JAMES G. HOLLANDSWORTH, JR.

LOUISIANA STATE
UNIVERSITY PRESS

Baton Rouge

Designer: Amanda McDonald Key
Typeface: Sabon
Typesetter: Impressions, A Division of Edwards Brothers
Printer and binder: Thomson-Shore, Inc.

The author is grateful to Thomas M. Paine and the Massachusetts Historical Society for permission to quote from the letters of Charles J. Paine. The author also wishes to thank the following collections and depositories for permission to use excerpts from unpublished material: the Historic New Orleans Collection, New Orleans, La., for permission to quote from MS 280 and the Charles Bennett Letters; the Louisiana and Lower Mississippi Valley Collections, LSU Libraries, LSU, Baton Rouge, for permission to quote from the Anson D. Fessenden Papers, the John H. Guild Letters, and the Henry Johnston Letter; the Massachusetts Historical Society, for permission to quote from the William H. Eastman Papers, the Dwight Family Papers, and the Civil War Correspondence (Lorin L. Dame Diary, James Miller Diary); the Minnesota Historical Society, for permission to quote from the Willoughby Babcock and Family Papers; the New-York Historical Society, for permission to quote from the Misc. Mss., Wilkinson, R. F., Manuscript Dept.; and Howard-Tilton Memorial Library, Tulane University Libraries, New Orleans, for permission to quote from the Civil War Letters, 1862–63, Civil War Manuscripts Series.

Library of Congress Cataloging-in-Publication Data

Hollandsworth, James G.
    The Louisiana Native Guards : the Black military experience during
the Civil War / James G. Hollandsworth, Jr.
        p. cm.
    Includes bibliographical references and index.
    ISBN 0-8071-1939-3 (cloth)   ISBN 0-8071-2336-6 (paper)
    1. Louisiana—History—Civil War, 1861–1865—Participation, Afro-
American.   2. Afro-American soldiers—Louisiana—History—19th
century.   3. United States—History—Civil War, 1861–1865—
Participation, Afro-American.   4. Louisiana—Militia—History—19th
century.   I. Title.
E540.N3H65 1995
973.7′415′09763—dc20   95-34787
                                                                     CIP

For Susan Hunt Hollandsworth

CONTENTS

Acknowledgments   xi

Abbreviations   xiii

1 Defenders of the Native Land   1

2 Great Pride in the Business   12

3 Woe to Any Man Who Flinches   23

4 When Tried, They Will Not Be Found Wanting   36

5 I Regard It as an Experiment   48

6 The Equal of Any "Yankee Troops" You Will Find   59

7 Unsuited for This Duty   70

8 We Shall Eventually Come Out Ahead   84

9 Diggers and Drudges   94

10 Manhood of the Colored Race   104

Appendix: Black Officers in the Native Guards   117

Bibliography   125

Index   135

ILLUSTRATIONS

following p. 52

Corps d'Afrique at Port Hudson

Sketch of black line officers, *Harper's Weekly*

P. B. S. Pinchback

Union commanders of the Native Guards

Companies disembarking at Fort McComb

View of Ship Island, Mississippi

The approach to Port Hudson

Confederate earthworks at Port Hudson

Depiction of the Native Guards' assault at Port Hudson

Captain Cailloux's funeral procession

Union camp and fortifications at Port Hudson

General Andrews' headquarters

School for black soldiers and freedmen

Colonel Quincy standing on the porch

ILLUSTRATIONS

Colonel Dickey seated on a sleigh

Black sentinel on a parapet

Corporal's Guard of black soldiers

Black engineer troops working on entrenchments

MAPS

Louisiana during the Civil War   *facing p. 1*

The Native Guards' assault on Port Hudson   *facing p. 53*

ACKNOWLEDGMENTS

Many persons have helped me with the research for this book. I would like to acknowledge in particular the assistance of Mike Musick, Mike Meier, Bill Lind, and Stuart Butler, at the National Archives; Bob Melchiori, of Vienna, Virginia; Joan Caldwell and Bill Meneray, at the Howard-Tilton Memorial Library, Tulane University, New Orleans; Faye Phillips, with the Louisiana and Lower Mississippi Valley Collections at Louisiana State University in Baton Rouge; Virginia Smith, at the Massachusetts Historical Society in Boston; Gail Bishop, with the National Park Service at the Gulf Islands National Seashore in Mississippi; and Fred Smith, at Choctaw Books in Jackson, Mississippi. I also appreciate the encouragement, support, and counsel of numerous friends, students, and colleagues at the University of Southern Mississippi, especially Orazio Ciccarelli, Jeanne Ezell, John Guice, Stan Hauer, David Huffman, Brenda Mattson, Paul McCarver, Neil McMillen, Lisa Moon, Henry Simmons, Kristi Vail, and Andy Wiest. My thanks also to Betty Ruth Hawkins for her assistance in preparing the maps and to Brian Wright for his editorial work on the proofs.

ABBREVIATIONS

AAG   Assistant Adjutant General

AAAG   Acting Assistant Adjutant General

AGO   Adjutant General's Office

HNOC   Historic New Orleans Collection, New Orleans, Louisiana

HTML   Howard-Tilton Memorial Library, Tulane University, New
             Orleans, Louisiana

JCCW   Joint Committee on the Conduct of the War

LALMVC   Louisiana and Lower Mississippi Valley Collections, LSU
             Libraries, Louisiana State University, Baton Rouge,
             Louisiana

LC   Library of Congress, Washington, D.C.

MAHS   Massachusetts Historical Society, Boston, Massachusetts

MNHS   Minnesota Historical Society, Saint Paul, Minnesota

NA   National Archives, Washington, D.C.

NYHS   New-York Historical Society, New York, New York

OR   *The War of the Rebellion: A Compilation of the Official Records of the Union and Confederate Armies*

RG   Record Group

VHS   Vermont Historical Society, Montpelier, Vermont

YU   Yale University

THE

LOUISIANA

NATIVE

GUARDS

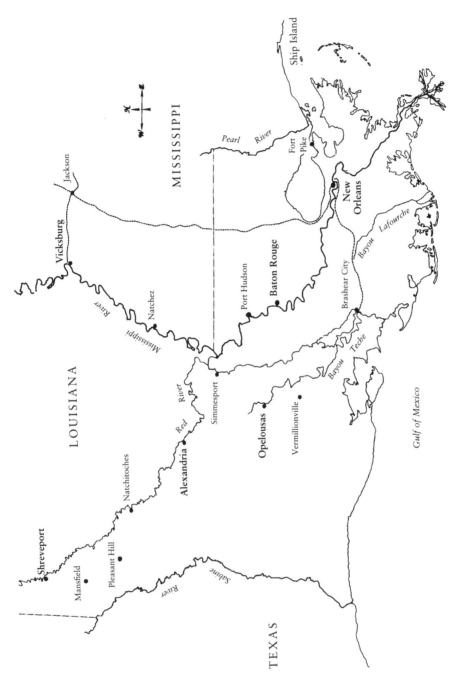

Louisiana during the Civil War

1

DEFENDERS OF
THE NATIVE LAND

It was a grand review. Twenty-six thousand men lined the dual carriage ways of Canal Street from the levee to the cemeteries, a distance of three and a half miles. "It was by far the greatest and most imposing sight ever presented by the population of the Crescent City," a correspondent from the *Daily Picayune* boasted. "Probably the present generation will never more see the like on the banks of the Mississippi river." [1] He was wrong, for the date was November 23, 1861, and the Civil War was just beginning. But what did make the event noteworthy was the sight of 33 black officers and 731 black enlisted men aligned in ranks alongside their white compatriots.[2] They were members of the Louisiana Native Guards—black soldiers in a white army, harbingers of one of the most significant and controversial social movements in our history.

The story of the Native Guards began seven months earlier with an announcement in the *Daily Picayune*. "Defenders of the Native Land," it read,

1. New Orleans *Daily Picayune*, November 24, 1861.
2. Elon A. Woodward, comp., *The Negro in the Military Service of the United States, 1639–1886: A Compilation* (AGO, 1888), 1027 (M-858, roll 1), NA. Three officers and 139 men were absent, bringing the total strength of the Native Guards to 36 officers and 870 men.

"We, the undersigned, natives of Louisiana, assembled in committee, have unanimously adopted the following resolutions. . . . : Resolved, That the population to which we belong, as soon as a call is made to them by the Governor of this State, will be ready to take arms and form themselves into companies for the defence of their homes, together with the other inhabitants of this city, against any enemy who may come and disturb its tranquility."[3]

In response, fifteen hundred black "natives" gathered at the Couvent School for Orphans on the corner of Greatman and Union streets to show their support for Confederate Louisiana.[4] "When . . . [they] form their regiment (and it will be a rousing one)," the *Daily Crescent* predicted, "they will make a show as pleasing to all, as it will be surprising to many of our [*i.e.,* white] population."[5]

Within days a regiment composed entirely of free men of color had been organized; it was called the Native Guards. Governor Thomas D. Moore accepted the regiment as part of the Louisiana militia on May 2, 1861, and issued commissions for the line officers, all of whom were black.[6] The governor appointed a white militia officer, Colonel Henry D. Ogden, as commander. White New Orleans was delighted with the formation of a black militia regiment. "Our free colored men . . . are certainly as much attached to the land of their birth as their white brethren here in Louisiana," the *Daily Crescent* assured its readers. They "will fight the Black Republican with as much determination and gallantry as any body of white men in the service of the Confederate States."[7]

3. New Orleans *Daily Picayune,* April 21, 1861.

4. The Couvent School was endowed in 1832 by Mme Bernard Couvent, a wealthy free woman of color, and was administered by the Société Catholique pour l'Instruction des Ophelins dans l'Indigence. The school opened its doors in 1848 to some two hundred pupils (Robert C. Reinders, *End of an Era: New Orleans, 1850–1860* [New Orleans, 1964], 139; also Rodolphe Lucien Desdunes, *Our People and Our History,* trans. and ed. Sister Dorothea Olga McCants [Baton Rouge, 1973], 21). It was probably the first free school for black children in the United States (Alice Dunbar-Nelson, "People of Color in Louisiana, Part II," *Journal of Negro History,* II [1917], 65). The school's principal in 1861, Armand Lanusse, was one of the "Defenders of the Native Land."

5. New Orleans *Daily Crescent,* April 27, 1861; also see the New Orleans *Daily Picayune,* April 28, 1861, and the New Orleans *Daily True Delta,* April 27, 1861.

6. Mary F. Berry, "Negro Troops in Blue and Gray: The Louisiana Native Guards, 1861–1863," *Louisiana History,* VIII (1967), 167; *OR,* Ser. I, Vol. XV, p. 556; Vol. LIII, p. 746; Ser. III, Vol. II, pp. 436–38. Unless otherwise indicated, all subsequent citations are to Series I.

7. Andrew B. Booth, *Records of Louisiana Confederate Soldiers and Louisiana Confederate*

Black soldiers in the state militia were not unusual in Louisiana, although they would have been everywhere else in the United States. Armed slaves and free men of color had joined the French in 1727 to fight against the Choctaw Indians. Eight years later, forty-five black men served alongside French colonial troops in New Orleans. Spanish officials continued the French practice of using black soldiers after the Louisiana Territory was ceded to Spain in 1762. More than eighty free blacks helped the Spanish army capture the English forts at Natchez and Baton Rouge in September, 1779. Even larger numbers of black soldiers, both slave and free, participated in the capture of Mobile and Pensacola six months later. When the Louisiana Territory became part of the United States in 1803, black men continued to serve in the militia. In 1811, they helped the territorial governor suppress a slave insurrection. Four years later, slaves and free men of color fought with Andrew Jackson at the Battle of New Orleans. As the *Daily True Delta* reminded its readers in 1861, among the current volunteers were men "whose fathers and friends fought in defense of New Orleans on the plains of Chalmette."[8]

Free blacks joined the Louisiana militia for varied and complex reasons. Charles W. Gibbons, a free black house-painter, testified after the war that he had entered the Confederate service fearing for his life. Gibbons claimed that other free blacks had volunteered from fear of losing their property, although he could not recall a single instance when that had occurred. Arnold Bertonneau, a prosperous wine merchant and one of the "Defenders of the Native Land," agreed with Gibbons' assessment. "Without arms and ammunition, or any means of self-defence, the condition and position of our people were extremely perilous," he told an audience in Boston several years

---

Commands (3 vols.; 1920; rpr. Spartanburg, S.C., 1984), III, 19; New Orleans *Daily Crescent*, May 29, 1861.

8. Berry, "Negro Troops in Blue and Gray," 166; Roland C. McConnell, "Louisiana's Black Military History," in *Louisiana's Black Heritage*, ed. Robert R. MacDonald, John R. Kemp, and Edward F. Haas (New Orleans, 1979), 34–46; John Walton Caughey, *Bernardo de Gálvez in Louisiana, 1776–1783* (1934; rpr. Gretna, La., 1972), 175; Roland C. McConnell, *Negro Troops of Antebellum Louisiana: A History of the Battalion of Free Men of Color* (Baton Rouge, 1968), 108–111; William C. Nell, *The Colored Patriots of the American Revolution* (Boston, 1855), 295–96; New Orleans *Daily True Delta*, April 23, 1861. Jordan Noble placed a notice in the *Daily True Delta* on April 27 calling for free men of color to serve as a home guard. Noble was a free black who had served as a drummer boy in the Battle of New Orleans (Nell, *Colored Patriots*, 296).

later. "When summoned to volunteer in the defence of the State and city against Northern invasion, situated as we were, could we do otherwise than heed the warning, and volunteer in defence of New Orleans? Could we have adopted a better policy?"[9]

Another reason why free blacks joined the Louisiana militia was economic self-interest. The Defenders of the Native Land were men of property and intelligence, representatives of a free black community in New Orleans that was both prosperous and well-educated.[10] There were even slave owners among its ranks. Not even New York City could boast of having more black "doctors, dentists . . . silversmiths, portrait-painters, architects, brick-layers, plasterers, carpenters, tailors, cigar-makers, &c."[11] Furthermore, the "hommes de couleur libre," as they were called in New Orleans, enjoyed privileges not afforded blacks elsewhere in the South, allowing them by 1860 to accumulate more than two million dollars worth of property. It was not surprising, therefore, that free blacks were eager to defend their holdings. "At this period in our history," a black Creole wrote many years later, "people were most cautious in their criticisms of existing institutions. The pursuit of personal satisfaction or the persistent acquisition of material things of life occupied them."[12]

9. Testimony of Charles W. Gibbons, December 25, 1866, *House Reports,* 39th Cong., 2nd Sess., No. 16, p. 126; "Dinner to Citizens of Louisiana," *Liberator,* April 15, 1864.

10. One of the "Defenders," Louis Gollis, was a forty-seven-year-old cigar manufacturer who owned real estate in the city's seventh ward (1870 U.S. Census for New Orleans, Louisiana, 7th Ward, p. 586). Armand Lanusse was a poet and leader of the city's black intellectual elite (John W. Blassingame, *Black New Orleans, 1860–1880* [Chicago, 1973], 13, 135; Desdunes, *Our People and Our History,* 13–17; David W. Moore, "Armand Lanusse," in Glenn R. Conrad, ed., *A Dictionary of Louisiana Biography* [New Orleans, 1988], I, 483; Reinders, *End of an Era,* 139, 219). Arnold Bertonneau and Florville Gonzales operated coffee houses, and Joseph Lavigne was a grocer (Charles Gardner, *Gardner's New Orleans Directory for 1861* [New Orleans, 1861]). McConnell, "Louisiana's Black Military History," 48.

11. Letter from Robert H. Isabelle to the *Weekly Anglo-African,* February 25, 1863, reprinted in Edwin S. Redkey, ed., *A Grand Army of Black Men: Letters from African-American Soldiers in the Union Army, 1861–1865* (New York, 1992), 252; also Arthé Agnes Anthony, "The Negro Creole Community in New Orleans, 1880–1920: An Oral History" (Ph.D. dissertation, University of California, Irvine, 1978), 28; Reinders, *End of an Era,* 23. The comparison with New York City comes from Ulrich Bonnell Phillips, *American Negro Slavery: A Survey of the Supply, Employment and Control of Negro Labor as Determined by the Plantation Regime* (1918; rpr. Baton Rouge, 1966), 438–39.

12. Finian P. Leavens, "*L'Union* and the New Orleans *Tribune* and Louisiana Reconstruc-

Fear and economic self-interest were not the only reasons why free blacks supported Confederate Louisiana. There was also the issue of self-identity. More than 80 percent of the free black population in New Orleans in 1860 had European blood in their veins. In contrast, fewer than 10 percent of slaves in Louisiana gave evidence of white ancestry.[13] Because skin color and free status were highly correlated, many free blacks identified more closely with Southern whites than with African blacks. "They [free blacks] love their home, their property, they own slaves, and they are dearly attached to their native land," read an open letter published at the time of South Carolina's secession. "The free colored population (native) of Louisiana have no sympathy for Abolitionism; no love for the North, but they have plenty for Louisiana; and let the hour come, and they will be worthy sons of Louisiana."[14]

An 1859 editorial in the *Daily Picayune* attempted to explain why free blacks identified with the white community.

Our free colored population form a distinct class from those elsewhere in the United States. Far from being antipathetic to the whites, they have followed in

---

tion" (M.A. thesis, Louisiana State University, 1966), 3; Manoj K. Joshi and Joseph P. Reidy, " 'To Come Forward and Aid in Putting Down This Unholy Rebellion': The Officers of Louisiana's Free Black Native Guard During the Civil War Era," *Southern Studies*, XI (1982), 327; Edwin Albert Leland, "Organization and Administration of the Louisiana Army During the Civil War" (M.S. thesis, Louisiana State University, 1938), 80–82; Desdunes, *Our People and Our History*, 19–20; see also New Orleans *L'Union*, May 5, 1863. For insight regarding the hopes and aspirations of the free black community from the time of colonial Louisiana to the present day, see Arnold R. Hirsch and Joseph Logsdon, *Creole New Orleans: Race and Americanization* (Baton Rouge, 1992).

13. Joe Gray Taylor, *Negro Slavery in Louisiana* (1963; rpr. New York, 1969), 162.

14. David C. Rankin, "The Impact of the Civil War on the Free Colored Community of New Orleans," in *Perspectives in American History,* ed. Donald Fleming (Cambridge, Mass., 1978), XI, 381; also Blassingame, *Black New Orleans*, 21; Reinders, *End of an Era*, 23; Charles H. Wesley, "The Employment of Negroes as Soldiers in the Confederate Army," *Journal of Negro History*, IV (1919), 241. For an extended discussion of the free blacks' rejection of their African heritage, see David C. Rankin, "The Politics of Caste: Free Colored Leadership in New Orleans During the Civil War," in *Louisiana's Black Heritage*, ed. Robert R. MacDonald, John R. Kemp, and Edward F. Haas (New Orleans, 1979), 107–46. For a point of view that rejects the importance of skin color as a factor in determining racial identity, see Hirsch and Logsdon, *Creole New Orleans*, 193–94. The quotation is from New Orleans *Daily Delta*, December 28, 1860.

their footsteps, and progressed with them, with a commendable spirit of emula-
tion, in the various branches of industry most adopted to their sphere. Some of
our best mechanics and artisans are to be found among the free colored men.
They form the great majority of our regular, settled masons, bricklayers, builders,
carpenters, tailors, shoemakers, &c. . . . whilst we count among them in no small
numbers, excellent musicians, jewelers, goldsmiths, tradesmen and merchants. As
a general rule, the free colored people of Louisiana, and especially of New Orleans—the "creole colored people," as they style themselves—are a sober, indus-
trious and moral class, far advanced in education and civilization.[15]

The degree of assimilation of free blacks into the white community was
such that Benjamin F. Butler commented on it shortly after his arrival in the
city. "In color, nay, also in conduct," Butler wrote, "they had much more the
appearance of white gentlemen than some of those who have favored me
with their presence claiming to be the 'chivalry of the South.' "[16]

Regardless of the reason, free blacks who supported Confederate Louisiana expected better treatment as a result, to move "a little nearer to equality
with whites," as one writer put it.[17] This hope was expressed on the day
after Christmas 1861, when Captain Henry Louis Rey rose before the staff
and officers of the Native Guards to give a toast. Holding his glass high, Rey
saluted "the Revolution which broke the chains of Young America, which
shook off the yoke of the Mother Country, and permitted her to take rank
among the first nations of the world!" Then Rey toasted "the present Revolution" and "all Revolutions—for they give birth to the progress of man,
and lead him on the way to true fraternity!"[18]

The first test of Confederate willingness to accept the Native Guards in
the spirit of true fraternity had not gone well. On September 28, 1861, word
had come that Union prisoners captured at Manassas would arrive in New

15. "Hayti and Immigration Thither," New Orleans *Daily Picayune*, July 16, 1859.
16. Butler to Stanton, May 25, 1862, *OR*, Vol. XV, p. 442.
17. James Parton, *General Butler in New Orleans: History of the Administration of the
Department of the Gulf in the Year 1862* (New York, 1864), 517; also see William F. Messner,
"The Federal Army and Blacks in the Department of the Gulf, 1862–1865" (Ph.D. dissertation,
University of Wisconsin, 1972), 62–63; and David C. Rankin, "The Forgotten People: Free
People of Color in New Orleans, 1850–1870" (Ph.D. dissertation, Johns Hopkins University,
1976), 296–99.
18. New York *Times*, November 5, 1862, translated and reprinted from the New Orleans
L'Union, October 15, 1862.

Orleans within two days. Their arrival was an occasion for much excitement, and the troops selected to guard the prisoners as they marched from the train station to the city prison would be afforded a great honor. General John L. Lewis of the Louisiana militia suggested that the Native Guards be allowed to escort the prisoners of war. But the Confederate commander in New Orleans said no, and white militiamen were picked instead.[19]

Despite the rebuff, the Native Guards continued to demonstrate their support for Confederate Louisiana by participating in two grand reviews—one on November 23, 1861, and a second on January 7, 1862. "Most of these companies, quite unaided by the administration," the *Daily Picayune* noted approvingly in January, "have supplied themselves with arms, without regard to cost and trouble."[20]

Enthusiasm among the Native Guards for the Confederate cause did not last long, however. Many of the men were still without uniforms or equipment, and one company had only ten muskets. Absenteeism increased when it became apparent that the Confederate authorities did not intend to provide the Native Guards with either the status or support they afforded white soldiers.[21]

The Native Guards were not the only ones who doubted the wisdom of

19. New Orleans *Daily Picayune*, September 29, October 1, 1861; Jno. G. Devereux to Lewis, September 29, 1861, *OR*, Vol. LIII, p. 746; also Ser. IV, Vol. I, p. 625. There has been confusion as to whether the commander who refused the services of the Native Guards was Major General John Lewis, the commander of the Louisiana militia (Berry, "Negro Troops in Blue and Gray," 169), or Major General Mansfield Lovell, the Confederate commander in New Orleans (Donald E. Everett, "Ben Butler and the Louisiana Native Guards, 1861–1862," *Journal of Southern History*, XXIV [1958], 203). Actually, it was Major General David E. Twiggs, whom Lovell succeeded on October 7, 1861 (*OR*, Vol. VI, p. 643). Devereux was Twiggs's acting AAG (Joseph H. Crute, *Confederate Staff Officers, 1861–1865* [Powhatan, Va., 1982], 196). Also see Arthur W. Bergeron, Jr., ed., *The Civil War Reminiscences of Major Silas T. Grisamore, C.S.A.* (Baton Rouge, 1993), 6.

20. New Orleans *Daily Picayune*, November 24, 1861, January 8, 1862.

21. Berry, "Negro Troops in Blue and Gray," 109; Joshi and Reidy, " 'To Come Forward,' " 328. In *Slaves and Freedmen in Civil War Louisiana* (Baton Rouge, 1976), p. 103, Charles P. Ripley cites a letter to document the growing demoralization of the Native Guards during this period. The quotation Ripley uses refers to the "shameful" behavior of "our young creoles" who "actually refused going out of the city for anything but camping" (Celly Nevins to "dear Sister Lou," March 2, 1862, in the E. C. Wharton Family Letters, LALMVC. A close reading of the letter suggests, however, that Nevins was not referring to black Creoles but rather to white Louisianians of French ancestry serving in the state militia.

having volunteered for service in the Louisiana militia. Many of the militia units organized in New Orleans were composed of foreign residents: British, French, Spanish, and others. They had come forward during the early months of the war to defend the city, but their loyalty was to their families and homes, not to the Southern cause. When the state legislature passed a law in January, 1862, that reorganized the militia by conscripting "all the free white males capable of bearing arms . . . irrespective of nationality," the foreign militiamen feared they would be ordered into the Confederate army. Governor Moore tried to reassure them that they would be used only for the defense of the city or as a local police force. Nevertheless, a distrust remained, which served to undermine the morale of the militia in general.[22]

The legislature's reorganization of the militia also affected the Native Guards. Because the new statute specified white males and disbanded all existing militia units as of February 15, 1862, the Native Guards ceased to exist on that date. Their demise was temporary, however, for Governor Moore reinstated the Native Guards on March 24 after the Federal navy under Captain David G. Farragut entered the Mississippi River.[23]

The presence of Farragut's fleet came as a shock to the Crescent City. At the beginning of the war, the Confederate authorities in Richmond had assumed that New Orleans was impregnable. The swampy ground that bordered the city made approaching it over land difficult if not impossible. Two strong forts seventy-five miles downriver, Jackson and St. Philip, blocked the approach from that direction. Consequently, Richmond had stripped the city of infantry to bolster the collapsing Confederate line of defense in Tennessee. All that was left to defend New Orleans was the ill-equipped and ill-trained militia.[24]

The Confederates also had underestimated their opponent. A Virginian

22. Act to reorganize the militia, January 23, 1862, OR, Ser. IV, Vol. I, 869; Charles L. Dufour, *The Night the War Was Lost* (Garden City, N.Y., 1960), 181–82.

23. OR, Ser. IV, Vol. I, p. 869; Woodward, comp., *The Negro in the Military Service of the United States*, 1033 (M-858, roll 1), NA; Orders No. 426, March 24, 1862, in OR, Vol. XV, p. 557, also in Ser. IV, Vol. I, p. 1020. Moore failed to transfer the Native Guards to the Confederate army, as he did some white militia units (Napier Bartlett, *Military Record of Louisiana: Including Biographical and Historical Papers Relating to the Military Organizations of the State* [New Orleans, 1875], 255, 259).

24. John D. Winters, *The Civil War in Louisiana* (Baton Rouge, 1963), 64–67, 77–80, 83–84.

by birth, who had honored his long career in the United States Navy by sticking with the Union, Farragut crossed the bar at the mouth of the Mississippi with a fleet of seventeen men-of-war and twenty mortar boats on March 18 and steamed upriver until he was in range of Forts Jackson and St. Philip. The awkward-looking but highly effective mortar boats were little more than flat-bottomed barges, each mounting a thirteen-inch siege mortar capable of firing a 220-pound shell. The high trajectory of the mortars enabled the barges to anchor around a bend in the river and lob their shells into the Confederate positions while staying clear of the forts' flat-trajectory cannon.[25]

On April 18 the mortar boats opened fire. For five days they pounded the two forts with high explosives and red-hot shot. The barracks, the hospital, anything made of wood in Fort Jackson, caught fire and burned to the ground. Rebel guns were dismounted, and the garrison was driven into the lower casements, which were flooded by high water on the river. During the night of April 20, two Union gunboats breached the Confederate boom of logs and chain that stretched across the river. After dusk on April 24, Farragut formed his seventeen warships into three divisions in preparation for a run past the forts. At two o'clock the next morning, Farragut's fleet moved forward. A small Confederate flotilla of converted steamers mounting light guns was no match for the Union men-of-war, and the guns in Forts Jackson and St. Philip could not stop the Union vessels as they churned past. All but three of Farragut's ships made it successfully past the forts that night.[26]

Once the Federal fleet was above the forts, pandemonium broke loose in New Orleans. General Lewis hastily turned over some obsolete muskets to the Native Guards and ordered the black militiamen to guard the east end of the French Quarter along Esplanade.[27] The mayor, John T. Monroe, begged the Confederate commander, Major General Mansfield Lovell, to evacuate the city rather than sacrifice it to the big guns in Farragut's fleet. Lovell agreed but continued to send men and supplies north on the Jackson Railroad to the Confederate training center at Camp Moore across Lake

25. *Ibid.*, 85–86.
26. *Ibid.*, 86–94.
27. "An Ex-Native Guard" to Chief Editor of *L'Union*, in the New York *Times*, November 5, 1862, translated and reprinted from New Orleans *L'Union*, October 1, 1862.

Pontchartrain, some eighty miles north of the city. Lovell left the militiamen to fend for themselves.[28]

At eleven o'clock Saturday morning, April 26, 1862, Farragut anchored his warships off the levee. The water in the river was so high that the guns of the Union fleet actually looked down on the city, making it an easy target for destruction. Farragut demanded immediate surrender. Mayor Monroe and the city council stalled because Lovell needed more time to move supplies and war matériel out of the city. Downriver, the mortar boats finally forced the surrender of Forts Jackson and St. Philip, which allowed transports to ferry the Union infantry to New Orleans. On April 29, a detachment of Yankee sailors, two howitzers, and a battalion of United States Marines officially took possession of the Crescent City.[29]

Lovell abandoned what was left of his supplies and headed north. Lewis ordered the Native Guards to disband, cautioning them to hide their muskets and dispose of their uniforms before returning home.[30] At least one Northern writer reported later that the Native Guards had been ordered to leave the city but refused.[31] Another writer claimed that the Native Guards had been ordered to blow up the United States Mint building when the Union navy arrived.[32] Neither assertion was true.[33] The Confederate authorities never

28. Winters, *Civil War in Louisiana,* 95–99.

29. *Ibid.,* 98–101.

30. "My Tardy Compatriots," letter from Captain H. Louis Rey, in the New York *Times,* November 5, 1862, translated and reprinted from New Orleans *L'Union,* October 15, 1862; also Lovell's report to Richmond, May 22, 1862, *OR,* Vol. VI, pp. 515–16; Berry, "Negro Troops in Blue and Gray," 169–70; Joshi and Reidy, " 'To Come Forward,' " 328.

31. Parton, *Butler in New Orleans,* 264. Parton's statement probably comes directly from Butler's testimony before the American Freedmen's Inquiry Commission on February 3, 1863, in Letters Received by the AGO, 1861–70, M-619, roll 200, frames 491–92, NA.

32. Joseph T. Wilson, *The Black Phalanx: A History of the Negro Soldiers in the Wars of 1775, 1812, 1861–65* (1888; rpr. New York, 1968), 183.

33. There is no evidence that Lewis ordered the Native Guards out of the city (Records of the Louisiana State Government, 1850–88, in the War Department Collection of Confederate Records, M-359, rolls 22–24, NA). As far as blowing up the mint is concerned, the only destruction of property contemplated by Confederate authorities concerned cotton and tobacco (see correspondence between Lovell and Secretary of War Randolph, April 23 and 25, 1862, in *OR,* Vol. VI, p. 883). Even after Lovell evacuated the city, he was uncertain whether he should burn the barracks and arsenal at Baton Rouge (Lovell to Randolph, May 1, 1862, *OR,* Vol. VI, p. 885). Given Lovell's desire to save the city from destruction by withdrawing his troops, it is unlikely he would have given the Federals an excuse to retaliate by blowing up the mint.

intended to use black troops for any mission of real importance.[34] If the Native Guards were good for anything, it was for public display; free blacks fighting for Southern rights made good copy for the newspapers.

34. For a discussion of Confederate policy regarding the use of black troops, see Wesley, "Negroes in the Confederate Army," 245–53.

2

GREAT PRIDE
IN THE BUSINESS

Federal troops under the command of
Benjamin F. Butler occupied New Orleans on May 1, 1862. Butler faced
numerous problems in the occupied city. Food was in short supply, and the
Crescent City's notorious lack of sanitation raised the specter of disease and
fever as the hot summer months approached. None of these problems was
more pressing, however, than that posed by the hundreds of slaves who fled
into Union lines. Abandoning plantations, they straggled daily into the city,
men, women, and children—thousands of mouths to feed.[1]

Some of the black refugees attached themselves to Union regiments, who
put them to work doing chores the men in blue disliked doing for themselves.
The 12th Connecticut Infantry, for example, had forty black women who
washed clothes and waited on the officers in addition to seventy men who
cleaned and repaired the regiment's barracks in the Custom House.[2]

Not all of the Union commanders were content to employ refugees as
cheap labor. Brigadier General John W. Phelps, an ardent and crusty aboli-

1. Winters, *Civil War in Louisiana*, 143–45.
2. John William De Forest, *A Volunteer's Adventures: A Union Captain's Record of the
Civil War*, ed. James H. Croushore (New Haven, 1946), 26–27.

tionist from Vermont, decided to increase the strength of his detachment by arming some of the fugitive slaves who had congregated around his bivouac at Camp Parapet near Carrollton a few miles upriver from New Orleans.[3] On July 30, Phelps asked Butler for "arms, accoutrements, clothing, camp and garrison equipage, &c., for three regiments of Africans, which I propose to raise for the defense of this point."[4]

Although Butler had used fugitive slaves, "contrabands" as he called them, to repair levees, widen drainage ditches, and strengthen fortifications, he had resisted appeals from Northern abolitionists to enlist them as soldiers in the Union army.[5] There were two reasons for his hesitance. First, Washington disapproved. Lincoln was afraid that arming fugitive slaves would push the border states of Missouri, Maryland, and Kentucky to side with the South. In fact, Lincoln had already forced David Hunter in South Carolina to disband the unofficial black regiment he had raised there.[6] A second reason was Butler's own opinion regarding the aptitude of blacks for military service. Blacks were "horrified of firearms," Butler had written Secretary of War Edwin M. Stanton three weeks after arriving in New Orleans. It would be "ludicrous in the extreme" to put weapons in their hands, he had asserted. "I am inclined to the opinion that John Brown was right in his idea of arming the negro with a pike or spear instead of a musket, if they are to be armed at all."[7] There would be no weapons or uniforms for Phelps to give the contrabands. Use them instead to cut down all the trees between Camp Parapet and Lake Pontchartrain, Butler told the abolitionist.[8]

Phelps was livid when he received Butler's response to his request. "I must

---

3. A Union soldier wrote his mother from Ship Island that "General Phelps is very much liked here by the men and hated professionally by the officers. He is a rough old bugger[,] seems to think just as much of a private as an officer" (John Guild to his mother, March 15, 1862, in John H. Guild Letters, LALMVC).

4. Phelps to Butler, July 30, 1862, *OR,* Vol. XV, pp. 534–35; Wilson, *Black Phalanx,* 183.

5. *OR,* Vol. XV, p. 440; Messner, "Federal Army and Blacks," 6–46; Salmon P. Chase to Butler, July 31, 1862, in Benjamin Franklin Butler, *Private and Official Correspondence of Gen. Benjamin F. Butler During a Period of the Civil War,* ed. Jessie Ames Marshall (5 vols.; Norwood, Mass., 1917), II, 131–34.

6. Howard C. Westwood, *Black Troops, White Commanders, and Freedmen During the Civil War* (Carbondale, Ill., 1992), 64–65.

7. Butler to Stanton, May 25, 1862, *OR,* Vol. XV, p. 441.

8. Phelps refers to Butler's order in his letter to R. S. Davis (Butler's AAG), July 31, 1862, *OR,* Vol. XV, p. 535.

state that while I am willing to prepare African regiments for the defense of the government against assailants," Phelps wrote to Butler on July 31, "I am not willing to become the mere slave driver which you propose." Phelps then tendered his resignation. Butler attempted to mollify Phelps by explaining the administration's policy about arming fugitive slaves. Only the president could authorize the use of blacks as soldiers, Butler informed his subordinate on August 2. Furthermore, he advised, "the arms, clothing, and camp equipage which I have here for the Louisiana volunteers, is, by the letter of the secretary of war, expressly limited to white soldiers, so that I have no authority to divert them, however much I may desire so to do." Phelps was unimpressed by Butler's rationalization and left New Orleans for Vermont.[9]

The incident was scarcely past before Butler began to have second thoughts about his refusal to enlist black troops. On August 5, a Confederate army under Major General John C. Breckinridge launched a surprise attack on Baton Rouge. Although Breckinridge's men were beaten back, there were ominous rumors that they were headed south to take New Orleans.[10] Butler hurriedly ordered the evacuation of Baton Rouge and sent an urgent plea to Washington for reinforcements.[11]

Butler had asked for reinforcements before, only to be turned down. Instead, the Union high command had told him to recruit new troops from the Unionist population in Louisiana, mainly the "loyal" Irish and German immigrants in New Orleans. Butler had tried to do just that, and although

9. *Ibid.;* Butler to Phelps, August 2, 1862, *OR,* Vol. XV, pp. 536–37; Ira Berlin *et al.,* eds., *Freedom: A Documentary History of Emancipation, 1861–1867,* Ser. II, *The Black Military Experience* (New York, 1982), 63–65; Wilson, *Black Phalanx,* 193. For further treatment of the Butler-Phelps controversy and Butler's decision to enlist black troops, see Berry, "Negro Troops in Blue and Gray," 169; Everett, "Ben Butler and the Louisiana Native Guards," 202–17; Louis S. Gerteis, *From Contraband to Freedman: Federal Policy Toward Southern Blacks, 1861–1865* (Westport, Conn., 1973), 68–71; Messner, "Federal Army and Blacks," 29–38; Ripley, *Slaves and Freedmen in Civil War Louisiana,* 29–32; and Westwood, *Black Troops,* 37–52.

10. Butler's testimony before the American Freedmen's Inquiry Commission, November 28, 186[3], M-619, roll 200, frames 0490–92, NA; also see Winters, *Civil War in Louisiana,* 123. An abridged version of Butler's testimony before the Freedmen's Inquiry Commission was printed in the New Orleans *Daily Picayune,* May 27, 1863. It also appeared in E. S. S. Rouse, *The Bugle Blast: or, Spirit of the Conflict* (Philadelphia, 1864), 155–58, and in Woodward, comp., *The Negro in the Military Service of the United States,* 2558 (M-858, roll 3), NA.

11. Butler to Stanton, August 16, 1862, *OR,* Vol. XV, pp. 552–53.

recruiting had gone well at first, it had fallen off. The disruption of slavery had created a labor shortage, and the Irish and German laborers who were expected to enlist had been lured away by the prospects of higher wages in the civilian market.[12] If Butler were to get the men he needed to defend New Orleans, he would have to look elsewhere.

Butler knew where to look, but he still had to convince the administration in Washington. On August 14 Butler decided to test the water. Warning Stanton of an imminent attack on New Orleans, Butler told the secretary of war that unless he got reinforcements quickly, "I shall call on Africa to intervene." He was deadly serious. "I have determined to use the services of free colored men who were organized by the rebels into the Colored Brigade, of which we have heard so much," he wrote. "They are free; they have been used by our enemies, whose mouths are shut, and they will be loyal."[13] Before Stanton had the chance to reply, Butler did precisely what he had told Phelps not to do; he called on the "free colored citizens" of Louisiana who had served in the Louisiana militia to enlist in the United States Army, "subject to the approval of the President."[14]

In testimony before the Freedmen's Inquiry Commission a year later, Butler explained his decision:

I had read carefully two of the daily journals of New Orleans published since the rebellion, and I ascertained that they had raised a colored regiment . . . and I got hold of the order under which it was raised. I then found that one of the Captains was a translator in the Provost Court of German, Spanish, and French, Mr. Sauvenet. I sent for him, and asked him—(he was a colored man, hardly a mulatto)— "You were a captain in the colored regiment?" "Yes, sir." "Are the other captains of that regiment here?" "Yes, sir." "Why didn't you go away with the rest of the

12. Halleck to Butler, August 7, 1862, *ibid.,* 544; Parton, *Butler in New Orleans,* 516; Stanton to Butler, June 23, 1862, *OR,* Vol. XV, pp. 493–94; Westwood, *Black Troops,* 43; Winters, *Civil War in Louisiana,* 142; also Butler's testimony before the Joint Committee on the Conduct of the War, February, 1863, *Senate Reports,* 37th Cong., 3rd Sess., No. 108, p. 357.

13. Butler to Stanton, August 14, 1862, *OR,* Vol. XV, pp. 548–49; also see Butler to Stanton, August 16, 1862, *ibid.,* 552–53. Stanton did not respond immediately to either of Butler's dispatches, perhaps because by the time they reached him, Stanton was distracted by the recent Union defeat at Second Manassas and Lee's invasion of Maryland.

14. General Orders No. 63, Department of the Gulf, August 22, 1862, *OR,* Vol. XV, pp. 556–57.

Confederate forces, when they ran away?" "We didn't choose to go. The whole regiment stayed." "You had white officers?" "Yes, sir." [Sauvenet was probably referring to the field officers, Lieutenant Colonel Henry D. Ogden and Major Henry Bezou, because all of the line officers were black.] "But," I [Butler] said, "how came you, free colored men, fighting here for the Confederacy—fighting for slavery?" "Ah!" said he, "we could not help it. If we had not volunteered, they would have forced us into the ranks, and we would have been suspected. We have property and rights here, and there is every reason why we should take care of ourselves." "Didn't you do it out of loyalty to the Confederate Government?" "Not at all; there are not five men in the regiment fighting on the side of the Confederacy." "Are you willing to enlist on our side?" "Yes!" "Will you get the captains and other officers to come here, and see if you can find your men?" "Yes, sir." These men had been drilled but without muskets. They would not let them have arms, whether because they were afraid to trust them, or because they did not have the arms to give them. He brought in the captains and some of the lieutenants—fifteen or sixteen, I think, and I found them all very glad to take service with us.[15]

Butler was pleased with the solution to his dilemma. As Treasury Agent George S. Denison reported to Salmon P. Chase, "By accepting a regiment which had already been in Confederate Service, he left no room for complaint (by the Rebels) that the government were arming the negroes."[16]

On August 24 Butler issued an appeal for men of color to join the Union army. The response in the free black community was enthusiastic. Within three weeks Butler was able to inform Stanton that "I shall . . . have within ten days a regiment, 1,000 strong, of Native Guards (colored), the darkest

15. Butler's testimony before the American Freedmen's Inquiry Commission, November 28, 186[3], in Woodward, comp., *The Negro in the Military Service of the United States*, 2558 (M-858, roll 3), NA. For Captain Charles S. Sauvenet's account, see his testimony, December 22, 1866, in *House Reports*, 39th Cong., 2nd Sess., No. 16, p. 44. The spelling of Sauvenet's name comes from the *Official Army Register of the Volunteer Force of the United States Army for the Year 1861, '62, '63, '64, '65* (1865; rpr., 10 vols. Gaithersburg, Md., 1987, VIII, 248) rather than the House Report, in which names were spelled phonetically from oral testimony. The New Orleans *Daily Picayune*, January 28, 1871, spells his name Sauvinet.

16. George S. Denison to Chase, September 9, 1862, in Salmon P. Chase, "Diary and Correspondence of Salmon P. Chase," *Annual Report of the American Historical Association: The Year 1902* (16 vols. in 24 parts; Washington, D.C., 1903), II, 313; also in Butler, *Private and Official Correspondence*, II, 270–71.

of whom is about the complexion of the late Mr. [Daniel] Webster." [17] The new regiment would be composed "altogether of free men," he reported.[18] On September 27, 1862, the 1st Regiment of the Native Guards was mustered into the service for three years and thus became the first officially sanctioned regiment of black soldiers in the Union army.[19] Butler named an assistant provost marshal from New York, Captain Spencer H. Stafford, to command the new regiment.[20]

Butler's account of the circumstances surrounding the reorganization of the Native Guards was not completely accurate. Officers from the Louisiana Native Guards had approached Butler first, rather than his approaching them.[21] Shortly after occupying the city, Butler had issued a proclamation ordering all citizens to surrender their arms. The officers of the Louisiana Native Guards had obeyed Lewis' orders when Confederate forces evacuated the city and hid their old muskets, some in Economy Hall, some in Claiborne Hall, and even a few in the Couvent School for Orphans. After the Union army arrived, a committee composed of Captains Henry Louis Rey and Ed-

17. Denison to Chase, August 26, 1862, in Chase, "Diary and Correspondence," 311; Butler to Stanton, [September, n.d.] 1862, *OR,* Vol. XV, p. 559.

18. New Orleans *Daily Picayune,* May 27, 1863.

19. Compiled Records Showing Service of Military Units in Volunteer Union Organizations, 73rd Inf. USCT, M-594, roll 213, NA. Major General David Hunter raised his unofficial regiment of black men at Hilton Head, South Carolina, during the spring of 1862 but disbanded the unit on August 9, two weeks before Butler's call for black recruits (Westwood, *Black Troops,* 58–65). A "Black Brigade" was also organized in September, 1862, in Cincinnati, Ohio, to construct fortifications. The three regiments that constituted this brigade were neither armed nor given uniforms, and when the threat of a Confederate invasion ended, they were disbanded (William A. Gladstone, *United States Colored Troops, 1863–1867* [Gettysburg, Pa., 1990], 21). Senator Jim Lane began recruiting the 1st Regiment of Kansas Colored Volunteers in August, 1862. Although this regiment engaged in combat as early as October, 1862, it was not mustered into Federal service until January 13, 1863, making it the fourth black regiment to enter the United States Army (Dudley Taylor Cornish, *The Sable Arm: Negro Troops in the Union Army, 1861–1865* [New York, 1966], 74–78). The famous 54th Massachusetts Infantry did not complete its organization until May 13, 1863, almost eight months after the 1st Regiment of the Native Guards was sworn into service (*Official Army Register,* VIII, 313).

20. Berry, "Negro Troops in Blue and Gray," 174.

21. Apparently, officers from the Louisiana Native Guards had approached Phelps in late July and asked about raising a regiment of free men of color. Having already been rebuffed by Butler, Phelps referred them to the department commander (Phelps to Butler, August 2, 1862, reprinted in Berlin *et al.,* eds., *Freedom,* Ser. II, 64).

gar Davis and Lieutenants Eugene Rapp and Octave Rey went to Charles S. Sauvenet, who arranged for them to meet with Butler to surrender the weapons and to determine what steps should be taken to demobilize the Native Guards. It was at this meeting that Butler raised the question of their allegiance. The four officers withdrew to discuss their options with friends and comrades. According to their version of events, Captain Henry L. Rey returned to Butler's headquarters on August 15 to confirm their loyalty to the Union. Only then did Butler decide to reorganize the Louisiana Native Guards for service in the Union army.[22]

Butler was also in error when he claimed that the new regiment was composed "altogether of freed men."[23] Only 11 percent (108 men) of the 1st Regiment of Butler's Native Guards had served in the militia. Although some free blacks who had avoided service in the Louisiana militia did join, Butler's Native Guards were primarily contrabands who found their way into Union lines.[24] "Nobody inquires whether the recruit is (or has been) a slave," Denison wrote to Chase. "As a consequence the boldest and finest fugitives have enlisted."[25] Black historian Joseph T. Wilson later estimated that more than half of the regiment was composed of fugitive slaves.[26]

Butler really did not care. Forgetting his earlier assessment of the blacks' potential for soldiering, Butler congratulated himself after the fact for having enlisted them in the Union army. "Better soldiers never shouldered a musket," he wrote in his memoirs thirty years later. "They were intelligent, obedient, highly appreciative of their position, and fully maintained its dignity." But even then, Butler's assessment was prejudicial, for he believed that black men were naturally more subservient than whites. "They learned to handle arms and to march more rapidly than the most intelligent white men," Butler

22. Desdunes, *Our People and Our History*, 118–19.

23. New Orleans *Daily Picayune*, May 27, 1863.

24. Denison to Chase, March 31, 1863, in Chase, "Diary and Correspondence," 379; Everett, "Ben Butler and the Louisiana Native Guards," 216–17; John M. Stanyan, *A History of the Eighth Regiment of New Hampshire Volunteers: Including Its Service as Infantry, Second N.H. Cavalry, and Veteran Battalion* (Concord, N.H., 1892), 156. Some of the black officers prided themselves in being able to recruit free men of color rather than relying on contrabands to fill the ranks (see Captain W[illiam] B. Barrett to Brigadier General [Daniel] Ullmann, May 17, 1863, in Barrett's Compiled Military Service Record, NA).

25. Denison to Chase, September 9, 1862, Chase, "Diary and Correspondence," 313.

26. Wilson, *Black Phalanx*, 195.

noted, because "from childhood up, the word of command had been implicitly and abjectly obeyed by the negro. His master's voice was his perfect guide." [27]

Butler's condescending attitude was typical for the time, even among educated persons who did not object to enlisting black soldiers in the army. A European officer on a visit to a Union army camp in Louisiana thought that black soldiers "will surpass any we have in our army" in their receptivity to discipline. Familiarity between officers and men arising from a common social background, which undercut discipline among white volunteers, did not apply to black soldiers. "Toward the black man we feel none of these delicate sentiments of equality," the European visitor remarked, "and he [the black man], on his part, has always been accustomed to be commanded." [28]

Butler may have allowed black men to join the army, but he did not intend to let them fight. This revelation came as something of a shock to John William De Forest, a well-educated and well-traveled captain in the 12th Connecticut Infantry, who fancied a colonelcy in one of Butler's new regiments of black troops. De Forest had met one of the black officers, Captain Francis E. Dumas, at a dinner party and had come away impressed by the culture and intelligence of the free black community in New Orleans. Several days later, De Forest approached Butler about securing a commission in the Native Guards. Butler invited De Forest to dinner but painted such a bleak picture of how he intended to use his black troops that De Forest abandoned the idea. Reflecting a stereotype that blacks were immune to the diseases of tropical climes, Butler told De Forest that he planned to use the Native Guards for garrison duty around New Orleans and other "unhealthy positions" and for "fatigue duty, such as making roads, building bridges and draining marshes." It was unlikely that black troops would be used in battle, and consequently there would be little opportunity for a promising officer like De Forest to gain distinction or promotion. "I advise you not to make your proposed application," Butler told a surprised De Forest, "for I fear it might be successful." [29]

27. Benjamin Franklin Butler, *Butler's Book: Autobiography and Personal Reminiscences of Major General Benj[.] F[.] Butler* (Boston, 1892), 493–94.

28. Wilson, *Black Phalanx,* 526.

29. De Forest, *Volunteer's Adventures,* 47–48, 50–51. Dumas became a major in the 2nd Regiment when it was organized in October, 1862. He held that rank until Banks's purge of black officers in July, 1863 (*Official Army Register,* VIII, 246, 248).

Unaware of Butler's deceit, new recruits continued to respond to his call to arms. They were quartered in the Judah Touro Building at the corner of Front and Levee streets, "a large unfinished edifice . . . intended[,] when finished[,] to be a refuge for indigent women and children." A reporter for the New York *Times* inspected the barracks while the Native Guards were being organized. Walking through the building, he was "much surprised to see how comfortably 1,700 men had found themselves." Commenting on the unappetizing military rations, the reporter noted that the Native Guards ate better than a majority of the white Union soldiers in New Orleans because some of the recruits had been professional cooks before they enlisted. He noted that the new black troops "learn the drill easily, and take great pride in the business."[30]

Recruitment for Butler's Native Guards continued at a rapid pace into October. It soon became evident, however, that there were not enough free men of color or contrabands willing to enlist to satisfy Butler's manpower needs. Consequently, Butler used two different but equally effective legal maneuvers to obtain local slaves for the Union ranks. The first strategy involved the Confiscation Act, which the United States Congress had passed on July 17, 1862. The Confiscation Act empowered military commanders in the field to confiscate property of Confederate officials or other persons giving aid to the rebellion. Butler reasoned that because slaves were property, he could confiscate them for service in the Union army.[31]

Butler's second legal maneuver involved slaves owned by foreign nationals, mainly British and French, who resided in New Orleans. Slavery had been abolished in both Great Britain and France, and citizens of the two countries were prohibited by law from owning slaves in a foreign country. Knowing this, Butler cleverly ordered all residents in the city to register, indicating to which country they held allegiance. When British and French citizens affirmed their foreign nationality, Butler made his move. "According to the law of the country to which you claim by this register to owe alle-

30. General Orders No. 63, Department of the Gulf, August 22, 1862, *OR*, Ser. III, Vol. II, p. 438; "The Regiment of Free Colored Citizens," New York *Times*, September 29, 1862. For two eulogistic accounts (in French) of the new recruits' military aptitude, see New Orleans *L'Union*, October 8, 25, 1862.

31. Blassingame, *Black New Orleans*, 35–36; Westwood, *Black Troops*, 7–8.

giance," Butler told them, "all negroes claimed by you as slaves are free, and being free I may enlist as many of them as I please." Butler's two strategies worked so well that soon twenty additional companies had been organized. The 2nd Regiment of the Native Guards was mustered into service on October 12, and the 3rd Regiment was sworn in six weeks later. The 2nd and 3rd Regiments were made up almost entirely of men who had been slaves only months before.[32]

Despite the radical departure from his policy of accepting only free blacks so as not to be accused of arming slaves against their masters, Butler still did not have authorization from Washington to organize the Native Guards. In early November, Butler complained to the newly appointed general in chief of the Union army, Henry W. Halleck, that despite many communications regarding the subject of black soldiers, no one in Washington had responded. In the absence of outright disapproval, Butler concluded that "I must therefore take it to be approved, but would prefer distinct orders on this subject." Finally, Halleck took a position, albeit a passive one. "The whole matter [is] left to the judgment and discretion of the department commander," he conceded.[33]

Butler's Native Guards were now officially members of the Union army and were beginning to look the part, as evidenced by the 1st Regiment when it paraded down Canal Street one bright Saturday afternoon that fall. With flags flying, drums beating, and the band playing "Yankee Doodle," Colonel Stafford led his men down the broad avenue. Along the banquette, white New Orleanians stared with disgust.[34] They should not have been surprised to see black soldiers in uniform, for some of these men had stood for review in the same street less than a year earlier. But now these black soldiers were

32. Butler's testimony, February 2, 1863, *Senate Reports,* 37th Cong., 3rd Sess., No. 108, pp. 357–58; *Official Army Register,* VIII, 246, 248, 250; *Douglass Monthly,* January, 1863, 777.

33. Butler to Halleck, November 6, 1862, *OR,* Vol. XV, p. 162; Halleck to Butler, November 20, 1862, *ibid.,* 601.

34. [W. C. Corsan], *Two Months in the Confederate States, Including a Visit to New Orleans Under the Dominion of General Butler* (London, 1863), 39–40. For more on the reaction of white New Orleanians to black soldiers in the Union army see "From Our Special Correspondent," New York *Times,* October 1, 1862. In New Orleans, a banquette is a sidewalk.

wearing Federal blue, and the complexion of many made it clear that these were not aristocratic free men of color but recent bondsmen, the liberated property of white planters somewhere in the rural parishes. The Civil War had finally come to New Orleans.

3

WOE TO ANY MAN
WHO FLINCHES

When the Native Guards had grown to three regiments, Butler moved them from the Touro Building to Camp Strong at the Louisiana Race Track outside the city. A correspondent from the New York *Times* visited their new encampment and was impressed by what he saw. "Their conduct could not have been better," he wrote. "In fact, I have seen older white regiments with more regimental drills, that are not their equal." A white officer with experience commanding white troops agreed. "You would be surprised at the progress the blacks make in drill and the duties of soldiers," he wrote. "I find them better deposed [*sic*] to learn, and more orderly and cleanly, both in their persons and quarters, than the whites. Their fighting qualities have not yet been tested on a large scale," he continued, "but I am satisfied that, knowing as they do that they will receive no quarter at the hands of the Rebels, they will fight to the death." [1]

The men at Camp Strong were of different backgrounds, sizes, and hues.

1. Letter from James H. Ingraham in the *National Anti-Slavery Standard,* November 29, 1862; also letter from "Capt. H. L. R." [Henry Louis Rey], in New Orleans *L'Union,* October 18, 1862; "The First Louisiana Colored Regiment," New York *Times,* November 5, 1862; *Douglass Monthly,* January 1863, p. 777.

Captain Emile Detiége's company illustrated how the recruiting had gone in the 1st Regiment. Youngest among the ninety-eight enlisted men were Pierre Silvester and Eduard St. Cryr, both sixteen. The oldest was a fifty-three-year-old carpenter named Brazile Brown, Jr. Half of the men were under thirty, but twenty in Captain Detiége's company were in their forties. The first sergeant, Joseph Frick, was forty-three. The median height was five feet, seven inches. Young Silvester was the shortest at five two, while William Anderson, a forty-two-year-old bricklayer, was six three. About a third of the company was of unmixed African heritage, while another third gave evidence of having some European blood. The remaining third were mulattoes, described on the roll as "yellow," "fair," or "bright." Almost 60 percent of the men had worked in the skilled trades—bricklayer, shoemaker, and carpenter—before joining the army. The remainder had been laborers.[2]

Most of the new recruits for Butler's Native Guards were native to Louisiana, although the 2nd Regiment included two privates whose home until recently had been Africa. They were named Wimba Congo and August Congo after the region in Africa from which they came. They had been brought to New Orleans three years earlier on an illegal slave ship, the *Wanderer*, and sold as slaves to a planter on the west bank. When Butler's troops moved through the area, Wimba and August made their way to New Orleans and attempted to enlist in Captain P. B. S. Pinchback's company. At first Pinchback declined to take them because their English was difficult to understand. Another officer insisted, and Pinchback gave in. The two new recruits for the 2nd Regiment were soon regaling their comrades with stories of ancestors in Africa, their customs, their tribes, and their kings.[3]

Colonel Spencer H. Stafford of the 1st Regiment assumed overall command of the three regiments at Camp Strong,[4] while Major Chauncey Bas-

---

2. Regimental Books, Civil War, Descriptive Roll of Co. C, 1st Regiment, Native Guards (73rd USCT), RG 94, AGO, NA. Bearss's descriptive summary of Company E in the 2nd Regiment reveals a similar pattern of racial, occupational, and age characteristics (Edwin C. Bearss, *Historic Resource Study, Ship Island, Harrison County, Mississippi: Gulf Islands National Seashore, Florida/Mississippi,* in National Park Service, Technical Information Center, Denver, Colorado, Document No. 635/D45, 207–208).

3. Letter from Robert H. Isabelle to *Weekly Anglo-African,* February 27, 1863, in Redkey, ed., *Grand Army of Black Men,* 140–41.

4. Initially, Stafford was reluctant to take command of black troops, stating that doing so "was in direct conflict with all my former opinions, prejudices and political association" (Staf-

sett, an old-school abolitionist and formerly a captain in the 6th Michigan Infantry, took command of Stafford's regiment.[5] John A. Nelson, formerly a captain in the 30th Massachusetts Infantry, became colonel of the 3rd, and Nathan W. Daniels from New Orleans was named colonel of the 2nd.[6]

All of the captains and lieutenants in the 1st and 2nd Regiments were black.[7] The 3rd Regiment had both black and white officers, the latter recruited by Butler from the New England regiments serving in the department.[8] Twenty-one of the black officers in Butler's Native Guards had served in the Louisiana militia, but only eleven had held commissions; the remaining ten came from the ranks. Twenty-six of the officers who had served in the militia (70 percent) did not offer their services to the Union army, and of the twelve Defenders of the Native Land, seven joined the Louisiana militia but only two of these chose to fight for the Union.[9]

The black officers in Butler's Native Guards were, for the most part, an

---

ford to Captain Wickham Hoffman [Banks's AAG], February 23, 1863, in Records of the U.S. Army Continental Command, RG 393, Letters Received, Department of the Gulf, Box 5, NA).

5. Edward Bacon, *Among the Cotton Thieves* (1867; rpr. Bossier City, La., 1989), 160–61.

6. *Official Army Register*, I, 197, 274, VIII, 246, 248, 250; Bearss, *Historic Resource Study,* 207.

7. Berry, "Negro Troops in Blue and Gray," 175. Technically, this assertion is only partially true. The original muster-in roll for the 2nd Regiment lists a free man of color, Samuel Lawrence, as second lieutenant of Company A, but Lawrence did not receive his commission and was replaced by William S. Peabody, who volunteered from the ranks of the 8th Vermont Infantry (Peabody's Compiled Military Service Record, NA). Peabody thus became the first white line officer of a black regiment, as he pointed out angrily in his letter of resignation dated August 15, 1864. Lawrence was commissioned as a captain in the 3rd Regiment when it was mustered in a month later.

8. All the noncommissioned officers in all three regiments were black (Berry, "Negro Troops in Blue and Gray," 175). The black line officers were largely responsible for the successful recruiting effort. For evidence that commissioning black officers was for purposes of encouraging enlistments, see General Orders No. 154, Department of the Gulf, October 27, 1864, published in the New Orleans *Tribune,* December 7, 1864.

9. Comparison of the Confederate muster roll for the Native Guards (microfilm) in the New Orleans Public Library with the September 27, 1862, muster roll for the 73rd Inf. USCT in the National Archives, officer lists for the 73rd, 74th, and 75th Inf. USCT in the *Official Army Register* (VIII, 246–51), and the announcement in the New Orleans *Daily Picayune* on April 21, 1861. Bartlett claimed in the *Military Record of Louisiana* that Butler failed in his attempt to revive the Louisiana Native Guards because "only 50 of the old organization responded to the call" (p. 255).

impressive lot, representing the elite of the free black population in New Orleans. A newspaper correspondent found them to be well-educated and conversant in a variety of subjects, including civic affairs, history, literature, and politics. "I found on one or two occasions," he reported, "that I was conversing with men of no ordinary knowledge and mental capacity." Those of Creole ancestry were fluent in both English and French. One characteristic of this heritage was a light complexion, which reflected the relationship between skin color and free status that existed in New Orleans during the mid-nineteenth century. Several of the black officers "were, to all superficial appearance, white men," another correspondent reported.[10]

Francis E. Dumas was a case in point. The son of a white Creole father and a mulatto mother, Dumas was educated in Paris, where he assumed the manner of a sophisticated Frenchman.[11] Upon returning to New Orleans, Dumas made a fortune as the proprietor of a clothing store and inherited several slaves upon his father's death. Because Louisiana law prevented him from manumitting his human property, he treated them well and allowed them as much independence as he could.[12] Most important, Dumas refused to sell his slaves so that he could ensure their well-being. After New Orleans fell to Farragut's fleet, Dumas told his slaves that they were free and urged those who were of military age to join the Native Guards.[13] Dumas himself assumed a captaincy in the 1st Regiment but was soon promoted to major and assigned to the 2nd.[14] Butler testified later that Dumas was "a man who would be worth a quarter of a million dollars in reasonably good times. He

10. "The Black Guards at Fort McComb, La.," *National Anti-Slavery Standard,* February 14, 1863; Rankin, "The Impact of the Civil War on the Free Colored Community," 381; also Blassingame, *Black New Orleans,* 21; Reinders, *End of an Era,* 23; New York *Times,* November 5, 1862.

11. Thomas D. Schoonover, "Francis Ernest Dumas," in Glenn R. Conrad, ed., *A Dictionary of Louisiana Biography* (New Orleans, 1988),.I, 264; De Forest, *Volunteer's Adventures,* 47. De Forest described Dumas as having "the complexion of an Italian and features which remind one of the first Napoleon."

12. Peyton McCrary, *Abraham Lincoln and Reconstruction: The Louisiana Experiment* (Princeton, 1978), 90; Rankin, "Forgotten People," 302. Manumission laws were relatively lenient in Louisiana during the early part of the nineteenth century but became more restrictive in response to the growth of antislavery sentiment in the North (Anthony, "The Negro Creole Community in New Orleans," 20–21; Leavens, *L'Union* and the New Orleans *Tribune,* 6–7; Taylor, *Negro Slavery in Louisiana,* 153–67).

13. "The Advocate of the Republican Party," New Orleans *Tribune,* July 2, 1867.

14. *Official Army Register,* VIII, 246, 248.

speaks three languages besides his own, reckoning French and English as his own. . . . He had more capability as a Major, than I had as Major General, I am quite sure." This was a dubious compliment, considering Butler's career as a major general, but Dumas was indeed a man of accomplishment and learning. Dumas also knew exactly what he was fighting for. "No matter where I fight," he asserted, "I only wish to spend what I have, and fight as long as I can, if only my boy may stand in the street equal to a white boy when the war is over." [15]

Another free man of color who accepted one of Butler's commissions was André Cailloux, a cigar maker by trade. Cailloux was a splendid horseman and an excellent athlete. He had been educated in Paris, and his polished manners and confident air made him one of the most respected leaders of the free black community. But unlike most other free men of color, Cailloux's line was untainted by European blood. By his own account, Cailloux was the blackest man in New Orleans, a distinction he noted with pride. [16]

Like Cailloux, many black Creole officers in Butler's Native Guards were drawn from the ranks of the city's working elite. One of these was Emile Detiége, who had set aside his schoolbooks at the age of thirteen to follow the bricklayer's trade. When Phelps began organizing former slaves who fled into his lines around Camp Parapet, Detiége volunteered to drill the would-be soldiers. He was well-suited for this duty, having been instructed in military matters by his uncle, an old Belgian soldier who had served in Napoleon's army. In the evenings, Detiége became a schoolmaster, teaching the new recruits how to read. After Butler decided to follow Phelps's lead by organizing the Native Guards, Detiége enlisted as a private in Captain Joseph Follin's company. By the time the 1st Regiment was ready to be mustered in, Detiége had been promoted to first lieutenant. [17]

15. Butler's testimony before the American Freedmen's Inquiry Commission, November 28, 186[3], in Woodward, comp., *The Negro in the Military Service of the United States,* 2560 (M-858, roll 3), NA; Dumas quoted by Wendell Phillips in his speech "The State of the Country," which appeared in the *National Anti-Slavery Standard,* May 31, 1863.

16. William Wells Brown, *The Negro in the American Rebellion: His Heroism and His Fidelity* (1867; rpr. New York, 1968), 169; Joseph T. Glatthaar, *Forged in Battle: The Civil War Alliance of Black Soldiers and White Officers* (New York, 1990), 124; Felix James, "Andre Callioux [*sic*]," in Glenn R. Conrad, ed., *A Dictionary of Louisiana Biography* (New Orleans, 1988), I, 147; McConnell, "Louisiana's Black Military History," 48.

17. New Orleans *Weekly Louisianian,* February 20, 1875; "List of Officers 1st Regt. Louisiana Native Guard Free Colored," September 27, 1862, in Regimental Papers, U.S. Colored Troops, Box 44: 69th-75th U.S.C. Inf., RG 94, AGO, NA.

Some of the black officers in Butler's Native Guards were of African-American rather than Creole ancestry. John H. Crowder, for example, was born in 1846 to free parents in Louisville, Kentucky. After his father abandoned the family by running off to Mexico with the army during the Mexican War, John Crowder's mother moved to New Orleans. To help support his family, young John went to work as a cabin boy on the Mississippi River at the age of eight. After four years, Crowder worked his way up to steward, the highest position a black man could hope to achieve on a steamboat. Under the direction of John Mifflin Brown, who later became a bishop in the African Methodist Episcopal Church and trustee of Howard University, Crowder taught himself to read and write. When Butler started raising the first regiment of Native Guards, Crowder lied about his age (sixteen) and gained a lieutenancy, becoming one of the youngest officers in the Union army.[18]

P. B. S. Pinchback was another black officer with African-American roots. Born in Georgia to a white planter from Holmes County, Mississippi, and his mulatto mistress, Pinchback was irreverent, intemperate, combative, and confident—just the right combination for an aggressive company commander. After attending school in Cincinnati, Ohio, he worked as a cabin boy on a canal boat following his father's death. Eventually, Pinchback worked his way up to steward on a Mississippi River steamboat. He was working on the river when war broke out but slipped through the lines after New Orleans fell into Union hands. When Butler called for officers to help recruit the Native Guards, Pinchback was one of the first to respond.[19]

The presence of black soldiers at Camp Strong created a great deal of interest among the black population of New Orleans, who flocked to the camp to witness the drills, parades, and other aspects of military life. A reporter for *L'Union,* a French-language newspaper published by free blacks,

18. Joseph T. Glatthaar, "The Civil War Through the Eyes of a Sixteen-Year-Old Black Officer: The Letters of Lieutenant John H. Crowder of the 1st Louisiana Native Guards," *Louisiana History,* XXXV (1994), 203–205.

19. Debate on allowing Pinchback to take his seat in the U.S. Senate, February 4, 1876, *Congressional Record,* 44th Cong., 1st Sess., p. 887; William J. Simmons, *Men of Mark: Eminent, Progressive and Rising* (1887; rpr. New York, 1968), 759–61. Pinchback was born in Georgia while his mother was in transit from Virginia to Mississippi. Although Major Pinchback took P. B. S.'s mother to Philadelphia in 1835 or 1836 to give her her freedom, she returned with the major to Mississippi and continued to bear his children.

visited Camp Strong on October 24, 1862. He reported that the men exhibited good discipline and maintained a neat camp. An advertisement appeared in the same issue calling for more recruits to complete the organization of the 3rd Regiment. "Ralliez vous sous le Drapeau de l'Union," it read. Volunteers were promised $100 and 160 acres of land as a bonus for enlisting, but only $38 was promised up front; the rest was due "à la fin de la guerre." The pay was to be $13 a month, with an additional food allowance for the soldiers' families. A special appeal was made for men who could speak both French and English to serve as noncommissioned officers.[20]

As the black regiments at Camp Strong swelled in strength, pride within the free black community grew to the point that it cut across the traditional boundaries of skin color and race. "Come visit our camp," Captain Henry Louis Rey of the 1st Regiment invited in a letter to *L'Union*. "In parade, you will see a thousand white bayonets gleaming in the sun, held by black, yellow, and white hands. Be informed," he continued, "that we have no prejudice; that we receive everyone into the camp."[21]

Most white Union troops in New Orleans were not as broad-minded as Captain Rey when it came to accepting the black recruits at Camp Strong. Some of the white soldiers had no problem with their enlistment, noting that "the niggers had as good a right to be shot as anybody." Other views were equally cynical. "What's the use to have men from Maine, Vermont and Massachusetts dying down here in these swamps," a soldier wrote his family from Baton Rouge. "You can't replace these men, but if a nigger dies, all you have to do is to send out and get another one." Most white officers and enlisted men in the Union ranks, however, had difficulty accepting black soldiers under any circumstances. Charles J. Paine, an infantry colonel recruiting a regiment of white Louisiana Unionists, wrote his father in Massachusetts, "Genl Butler is organizing a free nigger regt, but don't let people think that mine is nigger."[22]

20. Berry, "Negro Troops in Blue and Gray," 176; New Orleans *L'Union*, October 25, 1862.

21. This translation of Rey's letter dated October 16, 1862, appeared in *L'Union* two days later and comes from Joseph Logsdon and Caryn Cossé Bell, "The Americanization of Black New Orleans, 1850–1900," in *Creole New Orleans: Race and Americanization*, ed. Arnold R. Hirsch and Joseph Logsdon (Baton Rouge, 1992), 220–21.

22. New York *Herald*, February 4, 1863; Henry Martyn Cross to his family, May 4, 1863, in William Cullen Bryant, ed., "A Yankee Soldier Looks at the Negro," *Civil War History*, VII

The reception afforded the black recruits by the white citizens of New Orleans was equally hostile. When the editors of the *Daily Picayune* caught wind of Butler's plan to enlist black troops, they did not hesitate to predict its failure:

> The unfitness of the negro for military service is known to everybody. If he were not naturally a very inferior specimen of humanity, so far as the strong qualities needed in war are concerned, his life of slavery and subjection would render the adult slave a very unsafe person to be entrusted with a musket against the man whom he has all his life looked up to as his master and superior. But it is not the inferiority of the negro, his natural dullness and cowardice, his great indolence, and his awe of the white man, which so entirely disqualify the African for efficient military service, as that still more serious defect of any sort of sympathy in the contest in which he is required or invited to take part. The vast majority of negroes are contented with their situation in life.[23]

Contented or not, the Native Guards soon discovered that the price of enlisting was steep. The black soldiers were relatively safe as long as they remained at Camp Strong, but their families were not, and whites did everything they could to harass the families of the new black soldiers. Some of the rations that had been promised to feed the wives and children of black soldiers were diverted to white families instead. Those that were delivered were "far below standard." Some wives and mothers of black recruits were arrested and locked up in the parish prison for "safe keeping," while others were harassed by the authorities because they did not have passes that were never issued. Because the black enlisted men had not been paid, some landlords turned black families out on the street for want of rent money. Even the wives of the black officers, who were more financially secure, did not escape the attempt by whites to disrupt black family life. It had long been the custom in New Orleans for slave owners to allow, even to encourage, marriages between their slave women and free men of color. The more prosperous free husband would either provide for his wife, releasing the master

---

(1961), 144; Stafford to Hoffman, February 23, 1863, RG 393, Department of the Gulf, Box 5, NA; Charles J. Paine to his father, September 10, November 12, 1862, in Charles J. Paine Letters (microfilm P-382), MAHS. Originals of this and other Paine letters are in possession of Thomas M. Paine, Wellesley, Mass.

23. "The Negro Enlistment Scheme," New Orleans *Daily Picayune*, July 30, 1862.

of that obligation, or pay the master wages for the privilege of having a wife live in his apartment. Some of the black officers in the Native Guards now found that accepting a commission from Butler meant prolonged separation from their families, for masters retaliated by terminating the arrangement that allowed the slave wife to be with her free husband.[24]

White opposition to Butler's use of black soldiers took several forms when the Native Guards ventured beyond the confines of Camp Strong. Taunts and jeers were the most obvious. One soldier reported that they were "hooted at in the streets of New Orleans as a rabble of armed plebeians and cowards."[25] The derision was intended to elicit an imprudent response, which whites could then use as evidence of the unworthiness of blacks to wear a military uniform.[26] Men of the Native Guards often obliged by assaulting whites who insulted them and resisting arrest when apprehended for minor infractions of the law.[27] On one occasion, a policeman attempted to serve a warrant on a black soldier at the Touro Building and was set upon by the soldier's comrades. Fortunately for the policeman, Colonel Stafford and some of his officers intervened before much harm had been done. Nevertheless, the policeman had to beat a hasty retreat without his prisoner.[28]

Most confrontations, however, centered around the city's streetcars. Public transportation in New Orleans was segregated. Streetcars for blacks were marked with a large star. The black soldiers resented having to stand on the banquette waiting for an overcrowded "star car" while cars half full of

24. Stafford to Butler, October 11, 1862, in Woodward, comp., *The Negro in the Military Service of the United States,* 974 (M-858, roll 1), NA; also Stafford to Hoffman, February 23, 1863, and Stafford to R. Irwin, January 4, 1863, both in RG 393, Department of the Gulf, Box 5, NA.

25. "Letter from a Colored Soldier," dated November 4, 1862, New Orleans *Daily Delta,* November 7, 1862, reprinted in the *Liberator,* November 28, 1862, and the *National Anti-Slavery Standard,* November 29, 1862.

26. Spencer H. Stafford to Butler, October 11, 1862, in Woodward, comp., *The Negro in the Military Service of the United States,* 974 (M-858, roll 1), NA.

27. New Orleans *Daily Picayune,* December 14, 1862, January 24, 1863. They also sheltered fugitive slaves in their barracks, protecting them from arrest (New Orleans *Daily Picayune,* October, 2, 17, December 16, 1862, August 15, 28, 1863; New York *Times,* February 23, 1863). Colonel Stafford complained that many of these arrests were "without cause or on the pretense that they [the black soldiers] were slaves" (Stafford to Hoffman, February 23, 1863, in RG 393, Department of the Gulf, Box 5, NA).

28. New Orleans *Daily Picayune,* January 23, 24, 1863.

whites rolled by. Colonel Stafford tried to convince the railroad companies to put more star cars on the street but to no avail.[29] In September, 1862, several members of the Native Guards boarded a streetcar reserved for whites. When the driver told them to get off the car, they punched him and attempted to break open the ticket box. In October, another soldier from the Native Guards was arrested for pulling a pistol on a streetcar and threatening to shoot the driver through the head.[30] Further incidents were avoided by a compromise that allowed the Native Guards' black officers to ride on streetcars reserved for whites. Enlisted men and their families would still have to wait for cars marked with a star. This gesture did not, however, relieve the tension between black soldiers and white citizens, leading an exasperated provost marshal to complain that the black troops were "too insolent."[31]

Hoping to defuse the racial tension resulting from the presence of black troops in New Orleans, Butler ordered the Native Guards to join an expedition under the command of Brigadier General Godfrey Weitzel to clear the area around Bayou Lafourche of Confederate forces. The main Union body was to march southward from Donaldsonville along the bayou while four gunboats from the Union navy sailed from Lake Pontchartrain to Berwick Bay in an attempt to cut off the Rebels at Brashear City (now Morgan City). Butler ordered Colonel Stephen Thomas to take his regiment, the 8th Vermont Infantry, along with the 1st Regiment of the Native Guards and two guns from the 4th Massachusetts Artillery, and march overland along the New Orleans, Opelousas, and Great Western Railroad to link up with the gunboats at Brashear City.[32]

Weitzel's three thousand troops boarded transports at Carrollton on the

29. Messner, "The Federal Army and Blacks," 75. S. H. Stafford to the Editor, New Orleans *Daily Picayune*, September 24, 1862.

30. New Orleans *Daily Picayune*, September 9, 23, 24, 1862. The soldier's name was H. Carter (*ibid.*, October 23, 1862).

31. "To the Free Colored People of New Orleans," New Orleans *Daily Delta*, November 9, 1862; New Orleans *Daily Picayune*, December 14, 1862. At least one free black reportedly believed that pressing for equal accommodations on the streetcars might "call down upon themselves [blacks] the just indignation and enmity of the white population" (New Orleans *Daily Delta*, November 9, 1862).

32. Butler to Halleck, October 24, 1862, *OR*, Vol. XV, p. 159; Richard B. Irwin, *History of the Nineteenth Army Corps* (1892; rpr. Baton Rouge, 1985), 46–48; Entry for October 28, 1862, in Rufus Kinsley Diary, VHS.

afternoon of October 24 and landed at Donaldsonville the next day. Opposing him was Confederate Brigadier General Alfred Mouton with about half as many men. Weitzel started his movement southward along Bayou Lafourche on October 26. Meanwhile, the 8th Vermont and the 1st Native Guards marched westward along the railroad. The black troops were excited over the prospect of confronting the enemy. "We are still anxious, as we have ever been, to show the world that the latent courage of the African is aroused," Captain James H. Ingraham wrote as the 1st Regiment of the Native Guards marched west, "and that, while fighting under the American flag, we can and will be a wall of fire and death to the enemies of this country, our birthplace."[33]

The men made slow progress. Grass had grown up between the unused tracks during the summer; it was so thick that the locomotive could not make headway. Also, Butler had ordered Thomas to open the road as he advanced, which made it necessary to remove the grass between the rails. Unfortunately, the troops lacked scythes or knives and had to resort to pulling the grass with their hands. As though they were weeding a garden, the men from the 8th Vermont and the 1st Regiment of the Native Guards got down on their hands and knees and pulled up the grass. Their progress was slowed even further by having to rebuild culverts and replace rails that had been torn up by the Confederates. It took them two days to reach Boutte Station, a distance of twenty-three miles from where they had started.[34]

Weitzel encountered Mouton's small army near Labadieville north of Thibodaux on the same day the Native Guards reached Boutte Station. The Bayou LaFourche split both Weitzel's and Mouton's positions down the middle, which meant that Mouton might be able to fall on one Union flank or the other before either could be reinforced. But Weitzel had converted two large Mississippi River flatboats into a pontoon bridge and floated it down the bayou behind his advancing army. This allowed him to concentrate his entire force against Mouton by crossing his men quickly from one side of the bayou to the other. Mouton put up a spirited fight but failed to stop

33. Butler to Halleck, October 24, 1862, *OR*, Vol. XV, pp. 159, 161–62, 167–70; George N. Carpenter, *History of the Eighth Regiment Vermont Volunteers, 1861–1865* (Boston, 1886), 69; Letter from Captain James H. Ingraham in the *National Anti-Slavery Standard*, November 29, 1862, reprinted from the New Orleans *Daily Delta*, November 7, 1862.

34. Butler to Halleck, November 2, 1862, *OR*, Vol. XV, p. 161; Carpenter, *History of the Eighth Vermont*, 69.

Weitzel's advance. Learning that Thomas' column was moving from New Orleans along the rail line to his rear, Mouton ordered his troops to retire across Berwick Bay.[35]

Mouton need not have worried. The 8th Vermont and the 1st Regiment of the Native Guards were still toiling slowly along the roadbed. Onward they pushed, pulling grass, straightening and spiking down rails, cutting timber in the woods along the right-of-way to replace missing sleepers, and removing trees and other obstructions the Confederates had placed on the track. By the middle of the afternoon on October 28, the troops reached a curve in the roadway around which they would find Des Allemands station. Colonel Thomas received a report that the Confederates had massed their forces at Des Allemands. Placing a platform car with two pieces of artillery in front of the engine, Thomas ordered both regiments to form a line of battle. The 8th Vermont was to attack on the right, north of the roadbed, the Native Guards on the left. The artillerists took their positions on the flatcar behind their guns.[36]

Colonel Thomas knew that the black troops had been in the army for only a month and was uncertain how they would behave under fire. He crossed the tracks and addressed the men of the Native Guards as they stood in their line of battle. They were about to meet the enemy, Thomas told them, and not a man must falter. "If one of you hesitates," he warned them, "I shall shoot him on the spot!" After reminding the black soldiers that they were fighting for the glory of God and the salvation of their country, he called for them to avenge "the blood that has flowed from the lacerated backs of yourselves, your mothers, wives, and sweethearts." Thomas ended his oration with a threat: "Woe to any man who flinches."[37]

The skirmishers moved forward as the train poked its flatcar nose around the bend. The rest of the men followed a short distance behind. But instead of a fight, they found a smoking and deserted station. The long bridge across the bayou had been burned. In their haste the Confederates had left behind four pieces of artillery.[38]

---

35. Morris Raphael, *The Battle in the Bayou Country* (Detroit, 1976), 43; Weitzel's report, October 29, 1862, *OR*, Vol. XV, pp. 167–70.

36. Carpenter, *History of the Eighth Vermont*, 69–70.

37. *Ibid.*, 70.

38. *Ibid.*

The two regiments spent two days at Des Allemands rebuilding the bridge over the bayou before pushing on to La Fourche crossing, where they linked up with the main body of Weitzel's army. Weitzel ordered Thomas' men to continue repairing the railroad as far as Brashear City. This involved rebuilding a second long span over Bayou Boeuf. Within weeks, they had cleared fifty-two miles of track, restoring nine culverts and rebuilding two bridges, one 435 feet long and the other 675.[39] For their first time out, the black troops had acquitted themselves well.

39. Butler to Halleck, November 2, 1862, *OR,* Vol. XV, p. 161; Carpenter, *History of the Eighth Vermont,* 71; Entry for November 14, 1862, Kinsley Diary, VHS.

4

WHEN TRIED, THEY WILL NOT BE FOUND WANTING

By December, 1862, the area between New Orleans and Berwick Bay had been cleared of Confederate forces. The 1st Regiment of Butler's Native Guards was posted in small detachments along the New Orleans, Opelousas, and Great Western Railroad with headquarters at Lafourche Crossing. The 2nd Regiment guarded the section of track closer to New Orleans with headquarters at Boutte Station.[1] The 3rd Regiment, however, was given an assignment that foreshadowed the primary employment of black troops for much of the war. It was sent into the fields along Bayou Lafourche to harvest the sugar crop.[2]

Maintaining discipline among the black recruits, who had been in the army for only a few weeks, was a matter of concern.[3] Although some mem-

1. Field and Staff Muster Roll, Record of Events, November and December, 1862, 73rd and 74th Reg'ts U.S. Col'd Inf., Compiled Records Showing Service of Military Units—U.S. Colored Troops, RG 94, AGO, M-594, roll 213, NA.
2. Berry, "Negro Troops in Blue and Gray," 179. Four successive mornings of heavy frost, a very unusual occurrence in south Louisiana at this time of the year, killed the sugarcane along Bayou Lafourche, making it necessary to harvest the cane as quickly as possible (Bergeron, ed., *Civil War Reminiscences of Major Grisamore*, 98, 101).
3. Some of the fugitive slaves who enlisted in the Native Guards did not expect to exchange

bers of the Native Guards had engaged in petty theft while in New Orleans, stealing oranges, chickens, and the like, now they were accused of much worse behavior. An officer in a New Hampshire regiment stationed at Thibodaux reported that "there are endless complaints of burning, stealings, ravishings, and lesser crimes" committed by soldiers from the 1st Regiment. "It is thought that Gen. Banks will have to disband them or put them under iron rule," he wrote, "or to garrison the black troops at some fort away from civilization."[4]

Soldiers from the 2nd Regiment were accused of plundering the countryside and entering homes to steal jewelry and other valuables in the parish of St. John the Baptist.[5] The black French-language newspaper in New Orleans, *L'Union,* charged that these allegations were groundless. Noting that "impartial residents" regretted the Native Guards' departure when they were redeployed to guard the railroad on the west bank of the Mississippi River, *L'Union* asserted that the controversy was created by whites who objected to the recruitment of black troops.[6] What depredations did occur were more likely committed by bands of freedmen dislocated by the war and unchecked by the collapse of civil authority in the rural parishes surrounding New Orleans.

The black officers did what they could to maintain discipline, sometimes using excessive force. On the morning of December 9 near Terrebonne Bayou, a new recruit in Emile Detiége's company, Joseph DeGruy, was slow to respond to Detiége's order to fall in for drill. Captain Detiége grasped the young man by the collar and shook him roughly. "Did I not tell you to come immediately," he demanded. "Don't shake me that way," DeGruy retorted. Detiége shook the man again, roughly, and then yet again. DeGruy thrust his hand into the captain's face to push him away. Angered, Detiége stepped back, unholstered his revolver, and fired. The first shot struck DeGruy in the

---

the whip of the overseer for the strict discipline of the first sergeant and subsequently deserted ("Unwarlike Darkey," New Orleans *Daily Delta,* October 2, 1862).

4. M. Fauconnet to Butler, October 3, 1862, in Butler, *Private and Official Correspondence,* II, 351; Lieutenant Dana W. King to a Nashua newspaper, n.d., reprinted in Stanyan, *Eighth New Hampshire Volunteers,* 156.

5. Affidavit of J. Burcard and G. Chabaud, December 22, 1862, in Ira Berlin *et al.,* eds., *Freedom: A Documentary History of Emancipation, 1861–1867,* Ser. I, *The Destruction of Slavery* (New York, 1982), 233–34.

6. New Orleans *l'Union,* January 29, 1863.

lower abdomen and passed downward on the inside of his left thigh. Stunned, DeGruy stood still as Detiége took aim and fired again. The second ball struck DeGruy in the left breast just below the nipple and pierced the right ventricle of his heart, killing the hapless recruit instantly. Detiége told a coroner's jury in New Orleans that he had shot DeGruy for disobeying orders. Not so, said the jurymen, who indicted the captain for murder.[7]

The Union commander in the area was Brigadier General Godfrey Weitzel, a young West Point graduate from Cincinnati and son of German immigrant parents.[8] Weitzel did not like having black troops under his command. "I cannot command those negro regiments," he informed Butler. "The commanding general knows well my private opinions on this subject." Weitzel was convinced that the presence of armed blacks would incite a slave uprising in the territory he occupied.

> Since the arrival of the negro regiments symptoms of servile insurrection are becoming apparent. I could not, without breaking my brigade all up, put a force in every part of the district to keep down such an insurrection. . . . I have no confidence in the organization. Its moral effect in this community, which is stripped of nearly all its able-bodied men and will be stripped of a great many of its arms, is terrible. Women and children, and even men are in terror. It is heart-rending, and I cannot make myself responsible for it. I will go anywhere with my own brigade that you see fit to order me, but I beg you therefore to keep the negro brigade directly under your command or place some one over both mine and it.[9]

Most white Louisianians shared Weitzel's fears and denounced the presence of black soldiers parading among their slaves. A few days before Lincoln's Emancipation Proclamation was to take effect, rumors of a black insurrection intensified. On December 22, 1862, several planters begged Major General Nathaniel P. Banks, Butler's replacement as commander of the Department of the Gulf, to withdraw the black troops from the region.[10]

7. Taken from two accounts in the New Orleans *Daily True Delta,* December 11, 13, 1862, and the New Orleans *Daily Picayune,* December 13, 1862.

8. Ezra J. Warner, *Generals in Blue: Lives of the Union Commanders* (Baton Rouge, 1964), 548.

9. Weitzel to George C. Strong (Butler's AAG), November 5, 1862, *OR,* Vol. XV, pp. 171–72.

10. Affidavit of J. Burcard and G. Chabaud, December 22, 1862, in Berlin *et al.,* eds., *Freedom,* Ser. I, 233–34. Nathaniel P. Banks was a Massachusetts politician and the first Re-

Banks responded on Christmas Eve by ordering seven companies of the 2nd Regiment to Ship Island in the Mississippi Gulf to guard military convicts and prisoners of war.[11] He posted the remaining three companies to Fort Pike, which defended the nine-mile Pass Rigolets connecting Lake Pontchartrain with Lake Borgne and the Gulf of Mexico.[12]

The 1st Regiment continued guarding the railroad, but Colonel Stafford was eager for a change of venue. In early January, 1863, he wrote Banks, asking that his regiment be brigaded with the other black regiments and sent into the field. Noting that the enrollment of black troops was unprecedented, Stafford argued that they "cannot be fairly tried in the present service in which they are engaged, and while scattered in detached companies." He went on to praise their aptitude for military matters. "The acquaintance which I have formed with the characteristics, mental, moral and physical of these men, satisfies me that I am not too sanguine in the conviction at which I have arrived: that when tried, they will not be found wanting."[13]

Banks responded to Stafford's petition by ordering the 1st Regiment to Algiers across the river from New Orleans. On January 11, 1863, a troop train carrying the 114th New York Infantry pulled in at Lafourche Crossing to relieve the 1st Regiment of guard duty on the railroad.[14] That evening,

---

publican to be elected Speaker of the House in the United States Congress. Banks was appointed to the rank of major general at the beginning of the war and had the misfortune of going up against Stonewall Jackson in the Shenandoah Valley, where he was severely thrashed at Winchester. After being whipped by Jackson again at Cedar Mountain, Banks was sent to New Orleans to replace Butler, whose rough treatment of foreign nationals was causing diplomatic waves for the administration. See Fred Harvey Harrington, *Fighting Politician: Major General N. P. Banks* (Philadelphia, 1948).

11. Field and Staff Muster Roll, October 12, 1862, to February 28, 1863, Compiled Records Showing Service of Military Units, NA. The seven companies on Ship Island were B, C, D, F, G, I, and K. They arrived on January 12, 1863 (Bearss, *Historic Resource Study*, 211).

12. Powell A. Casey, *Encyclopedia of Forts, Posts, Named Camps, and Other Military Installations in Louisiana, 1700–1981* (Baton Rouge, 1983), 152–53. The three companies at Fort Pike were A, E, and H (Bearss, *Historic Resource Study*, 211).

13. Colonel S. H. Stafford to N. P. Banks, January 3, 1863, Regimental Papers, U.S. Colored Troops, Box 44, RG 94, AGO, NA.

14. Field and Staff Muster Roll, January, 1863, Compiled Unit Records, 73rd U.S. Col'd Inf., NA. For a more complete description of the 114th New York Infantry's deployment along the railroad, see Harris H. Beecher, *Record of the 114th Regiment, N.Y.S.V., Where It Went, What It Saw, and What It Did* (Norwich, N.Y., 1866), 111–14.

several companies of Stafford's regiment held a dress parade for the new arrivals. Captain James Fitts of the 114th was impressed by what he saw. Fitts later recalled, "As I looked down the 'long, dusky line' and saw the soldierly bearing of these men, their proficiency in the manual of arms, and the zeal which every unit of the mass displayed in correctly performing his part of the pageant, the barriers of prejudice which had been built up in my mind began to fall before the force of the accomplished facts before me."[15]

Stafford approached Fitts as the captain stood admiring the display of military precision. "Now look sharply down that line," Stafford remarked,

and I'll tell you a thing that you haven't thought of. Sir, the best blood of Louisiana is in that regiment! Do you see that tall, slim fellow, third file from the right of the second company? One of the ex-governors of the State is his father. That orderly sergeant in the next company is the son of a man who has been six years in the United States Senate. Just beyond him is the grandson of Judge ——, of one of the river parishes; and all through the ranks you will find the same state of facts. Deplorable, you will say, but nevertheless true. Their fathers are disloyal; these black Ishmaels will more than compensate for their treason by fighting it in the field.[16]

After reaching Algiers, eight companies from the 1st Regiment proceeded to Fort St. Leon on the west bank of the Mississippi River at English Turn some fifteen miles below New Orleans. The two remaining companies, A and D, were assigned to Fort McComb, which guarded Chef Menteur Pass connecting Lake Pontchartrain with the Gulf of Mexico.[17] A newspaper correspondent witnessed the departure of the two companies from their barracks in the Belleville Iron Works at Algiers.

As the Colonel [Stafford] made his appearance, a loud cheer went up from them, which resounded through the immense building. When the command to fall in was given, it was instantly obeyed, and then they were ordered to seize their stores and march to the station. Such a tumbling of boxes, barrels, tents, and every kind of material, I never saw before. In *four minutes* from the time the first order was

15. James Franklin Fitts, "The Negro in Blue," *Galaxy,* III (1867), 251.

16. *Ibid.,* 252–53.

17. Field and Staff Muster Roll, January and February, 1863, 73rd U.S. Col'd Inf., Compiled Military Service Records, NA; Casey, *Encyclopedia of Forts,* 202, 111.

given, these 200 men from all parts of the huge edifice had fallen into rank, been dispersed, had each raised his great burden, and was clean out of the building.[18]

Impressed by what he had seen, the reporter approached Colonel Stafford. "You can see my men can work, sir," the colonel boasted, "though people say they can't fight." At that moment a captain came up, saluted, received an order, and returned to his business. "I understood you, Colonel, that all your line officers were colored men," the reporter remarked. "There goes one, at any rate, who is white." "Do you really think him white?" Stafford asked with a smile. "Well, you may, sir, but that man is a 'negro,' for he carries the so-called curse of African blood in his veins." The officer in question was Captain Edgar Davis of Company A. The reporter had been fooled by Davis' light blue eyes, ruddy complexion, silky hair, and great mustache of a sandy color, nearly approaching red.[19]

Companies A and D traveled by railroad to Lake Pontchartrain to board a coastal steamer for the short voyage to Fort McComb. "At 9½ a.m. we left the Pontchartrain Station by railway and the scene here was really affecting," the correspondent noted. "Women were there, of all colors, taking leave of their husbands and brothers—and some of the feebler sex with an amount of fairness and refined physical beauty that many a white woman might covet," he continued. "The same emotion at parting, the same hugging, and weeping, and kissing of little ones was observable that would have been met among the same number of Anglo-Saxon warriors parting with their loved ones."[20]

Back along Bayou Lafourche, the 3rd Regiment completed the sugar harvest and traveled by transport up the Mississippi River to Baton Rouge, where it arrived on January 24.[21] The appearance of the black regiment caused a stir among the Union troops already stationed there. "A splendid regiment, worth, I believe, any two regiments on the ground," one soldier

18. "The Black Garrison at Fort McComb, Louisiana," *National Anti-Slavery Standard*, February 14, 1863.

19. *Ibid*. Davis' widow was not sure whether her late husband had African blood in his veins when she applied for his pension after the war (Rankin, "Politics of Caste," 118).

20. *Ibid*. The same account appeared with illustrations in *Harper's Weekly*, February 28, 1863.

21. Field and Staff Muster Roll, January, 1863, 75th U.S. Col'd Inf., Compiled Military Service Records, NA.

in the 52nd Massachusetts wrote to his mother. "They are officered by colored men," he told her, "which, I am told, is likely to give great offense to the white officers here."[22]

A correspondent for the New York *Tribune* seconded the soldier's praise for the new arrivals.

> The more I see of our colored regiments, and the more I converse with our soldiers, the more convinced I am that upon them we must ultimately rely as the principle [sic] source of our strength in these latitudes. It is perfect nonsense for any one to attempt to talk away the broad fact, evident as the sun at noonday, that these men are capable not only of making good soldiers, but the very best soldiers. The Third Louisiana Native Guards, Colonel Nelson, are encamped here, and a more orderly, disciplined, robust, and effective set of men I defy any one to produce.[23]

But another soldier had a somewhat different reaction. "God help poor darkey if the Rebbels gets holt of any of them."[24]

Not everyone at Baton Rouge greeted the 3rd Regiment with enthusiasm. The colonel of the 133rd New York Infantry told his men "to continue in the performance of their duty until such time as the regiment is brought in contact with [negroes] by guard duty, drills or otherwise." If that happened, he promised to march them back to their camp so as not to cause "their self-respect or manliness to be lowered by contact with an inferior race."[25]

The colonel's prejudices were shared by the post commander, Brigadier General Cuvier Grover, who refused to recognize the regiment as part of the Union army and would not allow it to draw clothing, blankets, or pay. Commenting on Grover's treatment, a correspondent for the New York *Daily Tribune* noted that "they [the Native Guards] drilled well, marched well, kept themselves clean, [and] performed all their duties as soldiers. Nothing in the world is alleged against them but that they are negroes, and

22. J. F. Moors, *History of the Fifty-second Regiment of Massachusetts Volunteers* (Boston, 1893), 47.

23. Correspondent for the New York *Daily Tribune,* reprinted in Wilson, *Black Phalanx,* 526.

24. Henry Johnston to "Friend Raynor," January 28, 1863, Misc. MS 2466, LALMVC.

25. New York *Daily Tribune,* February 21, 1863.

have negro officers; hence the ill-will, the detestation, with which they are regarded."[26]

The volatile racial situation exploded within days of the 3rd Regiment's arrival when a black captain reported for duty as officer of the day. The guard was composed of white soldiers from the 13th Maine. When the black captain arrived to inspect the guard, they refused to acknowledge his authority. The white soldiers were willing to "obey every order consistent with their manhood," a correspondent reported, "but as to acknowledging a negro their superior, by any virtue of shoulder straps he might wear, they would not." The situation quickly turned ugly. The black officer pressed his authority; the white soldiers grounded their rifles in protest and threatened to kill him should he attempt to coerce their obedience.[27]

Nathaniel P. Banks, the new department commander, soon heard of the episode but did not punish the mutinous white soldiers from the 13th Maine. Instead, he ordered all the black officers in the 3rd Regiment to report to his headquarters in New Orleans.[28] Once they arrived, Banks asked them to explain what had happened. One or two spoke up about the problems they were facing as black officers in a white army. Banks said that he would take the matter under advisement and told them to return the next day.[29] During the second interview, Banks skillfully led the black officers into a trap. He began by telling them that it was the government's policy not to commission blacks as officers in the army. In light of their grievances, Banks recommended that they resign and thereby avoid the embarrassment of being

26. *Ibid.* The 2nd Regiment met with a similar reception when it arrived on Ship Island. Two companies on the island from the 13th Maine Infantry objected so strenuously to the presence of black troops that they had to be placed under arrest and transferred to Fort Jackson (Bearss, *Historic Resource Study,* 211–12).

27. Rankin, "Forgotten People," 182; "Colorphobia in the Army," *National Anti-Slavery Standard,* February 28, 1863.

28. Petition of Joseph G. Parker to Stanton, May 30, 1863, in Woodward, comp., *The Negro in the Military Service of the United States,* 1273–75 (M-858, roll 2), NA. Also see Robert H. Isabelle's letter to *Weekly Anglo-African,* February 25, 1863, in Redkey, ed., *Grand Army of Black Men,* 251.

29. *Official Army Register,* VIII, 246–51; Joshi and Reidy, " 'To Come Forward,' " 330; Moors, *History of the Fifty-second Massachusetts Volunteers,* 62; Joseph G. Parker to Stanton, May 30, 1863, in Woodward, comp., *The Negro in the Military Service of the United States,* 1273–75 (M-858, roll 2), NA; also Ripley, *Slaves and Freedmen in Civil War Louisiana,* 117.

"kicked out."[30] Uncertain over their future, the black officers agreed and offered a letter of resignation signed by all sixteen men. "At the time we entered the army," they wrote, "it was the expectation of ourselves, and men, that we would be treated as Soldiers."

> We did not expect, or demand[,] to be put on a Perfect equality in a social point of view with the whites. But we did most certainly expect the Privileges, and respect due to a soldier who had offered his service and his life to his government, ever ready and willing to share the common dangers of the Battle field. This we have not received, on the contrary, we have met with scorn and contempt, from both military and civilians. If we are forced to ask for information from the generality of white officers, we invariably receive abrupt, and ungentlemanly answers, when in many instances it is their legitimate business to give the Information required. To be spoken to, by a colored officer, to most of them, seems an insult. Even our own regimental commander has abused us, under the cover of his authority, presuming upon our limited knowledge of military discipline. All combine to make our Position insufferable.[31]

Banks was pleased to accept their resignations, and when the sixteen men returned to Baton Rouge, they found that white officers had already been named to take their place.[32] Realizing that they had been tricked, they asked to be reinstated. Banks refused, leading the officers to write Secretary of War Stanton directly. "Are we properly discharged?" they asked. "Are we liable to conscription?" All they wanted was a fair chance to prove themselves. "We are not wanted in this department," they wrote. "But sir, put us to the test of a board of examination, and if we do not pass we are satisfied to give up troubling the Authorities for positions."[33]

Richard B. Irwin, Banks's adjutant, explained the situation from Banks's point of view.

30. "Gallant Officers to Be Put into the Ranks," New Orleans *Tribune,* May 14, 1865.

31. Sixteen black officers (by name) from the 3rd Louisiana Native Guards to Banks, September 19, 1863, in Captain Leon G. Forstall's Compiled Military Service Record, NA. Four of the officers had served in the Louisiana militia as enlisted men.

32. For evidence that white officers had been appointed to replace the black officers even before they submitted their letter of resignation see J. F. Moors's letter to his wife, February 15, 1863, in Moors, *History of the Fifty-Second Massachusetts Volunteers,* 62.

33. Joseph G. Parker to Stanton, May 30, 1863, in Woodward, comp., *The Negro in the Military Service of the United States,* 1273–75 (M-858, roll 2), NA.

The arrival of the 3rd Louisiana Native Guards at Baton Rouge early in this year led to much ill-feeling among the officers and men of some of the white regiments, resulting often in controversy, and on several occasions in violence. By their arrogance and intolerant self-assertion, the officers of this regiment had conclusively shown that they were not men to pioneer this experiment, even before they proceeded to demonstrate their hostile and uncompromising spirit by seeking occasions to force their complaints upon the Dept. Commander. . . . Whatever may be the general merits of the question, no candid man can doubt that in its practical operation, the experiment of officering colored troops with colored men has . . . proved a distressing failure.[34]

The petition was forwarded to Washington, where it was shelved.[35]

Unaware of the controversy surrounding the black officers in the 3rd Regiment, the 1st Regiment arrived in Baton Rouge to join the 3rd on March 19, 1863.[36] Commenting on the black soldiers' muscular physiques honed by years of hard labor, a quartermaster's clerk in the 49th Massachusetts reported that they were "great lusty fellows, with breasts like women's; they take us down as far as brute strength is concerned." It was the Native Guards' proficiency on the drill field, however, that garnered his greatest praise. "When I contrasted their elastic, vigorous steps with our wan looks and increasing debility, I felt that they had not been recruited any too soon. Dressed in full uniform, they made a fine appearance, and marched as one man. . . . Properly officered, and they will make the *best* soldiers in America."[37]

The Native Guards may have had the potential to become fine soldiers, but the Union army seemed to be doing everything it could to prevent that from happening. The black soldiers were armed with obsolete rife-muskets

34. Irwin's endorsement on Parker's petition of May 30, 1863, *ibid.*, 1277–78. Apparently, Stanton ignored the petition, for the black officers in the 3rd Regiment were never reinstated.

35. Curiously, after the war, when the War Department compiled its register of volunteer officers serving in the United States Army, the sixteen black officers who had resigned from the 3rd Regiment were listed as "discharged" instead of having resigned (*Official Army Register*, VIII, 250–51).

36. Field and Staff Muster Rolls, March and April, 1863, 73rd U.S. Col'd Inf., Compiled Military Service Records, NA.

37. Henry T. Johns, *Life with the Forty-ninth Massachusetts Volunteers* (Pittsfield, Mass., 1864), 150.

of either American or European manufacture.[38] Lumber for the floors of tents and ammunition for target practice went to white troops. In addition, the equipment issued to the black troops was of poor quality. The uniforms were cast-offs from white regiments, the knapsacks lacked shoulder straps, and there were only enough haversacks in each regiment to supply one company. On top of that, the troops had not been paid, nor did they receive the bounty they had been promised when they volunteered.[39]

Despite these handicaps, the Native Guards demonstrated their aptitude for soldiering on April 8, when a detachment of 180 men from the 2nd Regiment on Ship Island boarded the transport *General Banks* for a foray to the mainland. After spending a night anchored off Horn Island, the *General Banks* rendezvoused with the gunboat *John P. Jackson* at daybreak on the ninth. The two vessels then set out for East Pascagoula, Mississippi, and by mid-morning had reached their destination. The *John P. Jackson* anchored twelve hundred yards offshore to cover the *General Banks* as she ran in against a long wharf near the town. Twenty men under Captain Charles Sauvenet secured the wharf, while the remainder of the detachment cautiously approached a large frame hotel. Entering the building, several Native Guards climbed to the roof and unfurled a United States flag. If they were hoping to provoke a fight, they were successful, for Confederate infantry and cavalry swarmed over the detachment. In a four-hour running battle, the black troops held their ground, repulsing several attempts to cut them off from the *General Banks* and suffering two killed and eight wounded. Learning that Confederate reinforcements were arriving, Colonel Daniels ordered his men back to the boat. While the black soldiers crowded on the wharf, the *John P. Jackson* provided covering fire. Unfortunately, a shell from a six-inch rifled cannon fell short and exploded, killing four and wounding five of the Native Guards as they scrambled aboard the *General Banks*.[40]

38. Bearss, *Historic Resource Study,* 224.

39. Stafford to Hoffman, February 23, 1863, in RG 393, Department of the Gulf, Box 5, NA.

40. Bearss, *Historic Resource Study,* 213–14; "L'Expedition de Pascagoula: Exploits du 2nd Régiment des Native-Guards," New Orleans *L'Union,* April 14, 1863. Sauvenet was the translator at the provost marshal's court who served as the intermediary for Butler and the black officers from the Louisiana militia. Daniels' report to Brigadier General Sherman, April 11, 1863, reprinted in Brown, *The Negro in the American Rebellion,* 163–66; also summarized in the *National Anti-Slavery Standard,* April 25, 1863.

This was one of the first engagements between black Union troops and Confederate forces in the Civil War, and the Native Guards had acquitted themselves well.[41] After holding their position under heavy fire, they retreated in good order, bringing off three prisoners and a Confederate flag as evidence of their mettle.[42] Although it would not attract the same attention as later actions, the engagement at Pascagoula demonstrated that black soldiers could and would fight. "The oppression which they have heretofore undergone at the hands of their foes, and the obloquy that had been showered upon them by those who should have been their friends," Daniels wrote in his report, "had not extinguished their manhood, or suppressed their bravery."[43]

41. Although at the time not officially part of the Union army, the 1st Regiment of Kansas Colored Volunteers clashed with some Missouri bushwhackers at Island Mound, Missouri, on October 29, 1862, giving that regiment the distinction of being the first black unit to engage Rebels, albeit irregulars, in combat (Bearss, *Historic Resource Study,* 214; Cornish, *Sable Arm,* 77).

42. New Orleans *L'Union,* April 14, 1863.

43. Brown, *The Negro in the American Rebellion,* 166. In his report, Daniels cited Major Francis Dumas for bravery.

5

I REGARD IT AS
AN EXPERIMENT

The major objective for the Union army in the Mississippi Valley in 1863 was to wrestle control of the Mississippi River from the Confederates. To that end, Ulysses S. Grant pushed his army slowly down the west bank of the Mississippi River, looking for a way to gain a foothold on dry ground below Vicksburg from which to launch an assault on the Rebel fortress. Nathaniel P. Banks was expected to make his way up the river from New Orleans to effect a juncture with Grant at Vicksburg, splitting the Confederacy in two.[1] The major obstacle confronting Banks was Port Hudson, a well-fortified Confederate stronghold clinging to high bluffs on a hairpin bend of the Mississippi River some fourteen miles north of Baton Rouge.

Banks tested the Rebel fortifications at Port Hudson on March 14 with a feeble diversionary attack while Farragut attempted to run past the batteries covering the river. The whole affair was a disaster; Banks accomplished nothing, and Farragut's fleet was badly shot up. Nevertheless, the admiral did make it past Port Hudson with two ships and was able to establish

1. C. Grover to Banks's AAG, December 17, 1862, *OR,* Vol. XV, p. 191; also Special Orders No. 29, December 15, 1862, *ibid.,* 609.

contact with Grant's forces near Vicksburg. The Confederate stronghold at Port Hudson still held firm, however, and Banks fell back to Baton Rouge to reconsider his options.

By early April Banks decided to bypass Port Hudson. Moving up Bayou Teche to Vermillionville (now Lafayette) and on to Alexandria, Banks dispersed all Confederate attempts to resist his advance. Having accomplished his objective of opening a water route to the Mississippi River via the Atchafalaya Basin, Banks abandoned Alexandria and marched his army down the Red River toward the Confederate citadel at Port Hudson. By May 22 Banks had crossed the Mississippi River and invested Port Hudson from the north, while Union troops from Baton Rouge sealed off the fortress from the south. The siege of Port Hudson had begun.

The 1st and 3rd Regiments of the Native Guards did not accompany Banks's army into central Louisiana but were left behind in Baton Rouge to fret over their inaction. As often happens when troops are frustrated by the dull routine of garrison duty, disciplinary infractions occurred. In late April, a local woman, who had nursed young Lieutenant John Crowder back to health when he was sick with the fever, visited the 1st Regiment's camp, accompanied by a young girl. A private soldier, probably thinking to shock the lady, unbuttoned his trousers and exposed his penis. Captain Alcide Lewis observed the incident but failed to discipline the man. When Crowder found out what had happened, he promptly had the soldier arrested, which made Lewis' inaction look like dereliction of duty. Lewis was incensed, but Crowder did not care. "My opinion of Capt. Lewis and Lieut. Moss has been reduced since my arrival in this city," he wrote his mother. "They are the most pucillanamous dirty Low life men that I ever seen. Like many others they have no respect for no one. they seem to think there is not a woman that they cannot sleep with. every woman seems to be a common woman with them. they have grown hateful in my sight."[2]

Two weeks later there was another incident, this one involving the 1st

---

2. Crowder to his mother, April 27, 1863, in Glatthaar, "The Civil War Through the Eyes of a Sixteen-Year-Old Black Officer," 213. It is not known whether Crowder's friend, identified only as Mrs. Marsh, was white or black. From Crowder's description, Mrs. Marsh was apparently well situated (Crowder to his mother, April 18, 1863, *ibid.*, 211). The 1860 census recorded no Marshes in Baton Rouge, although an "M. Marsh" resided in Port Hudson, just up the road. M. Marsh was a thirty-eight-year-old white physician born in New York.

Regiment's colonel, Spencer H. Stafford.[3] On May 13, a woodcutting detail from the 1st Regiment was stopped at the picket line because the men did not have a pass. The detail went back to camp and told Colonel Stafford what had happened. Stafford returned with his men and rode up to the officer of the guard, Captain J. P. Garland of the 21st Maine Infantry. "What in hell did you stop my teams for?" Stafford demanded. Garland replied that he was following orders. "You are a God damned pusillanimous, stinking[,] white-livered Yankee," Stafford retorted, shaking his fist in the captain's face. "You stopped my men so that some of your Regt could steal my wood," Stafford charged. Garland responded that his orders came from Colonel Edward P. Chapin, the brigade commander. "Yes," Stafford replied, "I have heard of that Brigade before and they are a set of God damn thieves." Garland held his tongue while Stafford continued his tirade but had the presence of mind to take out a notebook and record the colonel's remarks. Seeing what Garland was doing, Stafford slacked his anger and left with his men.[4]

Captain Garland immediately informed Colonel Chapin of what had happened. Chapin told Banks, and Banks ordered Stafford placed under arrest. In a letter protesting his detention, Stafford complained that the guard at the picket line had treated the black officer in charge of the detail roughly, calling him a "black son of a bitch." Stafford said that he was angered by the affront, for it was not the first time the men of his command had been so treated. "This excited my indignation unduly I confess, and I used expressions which I regretted as soon as I returned to camp and had time to reflect." Nonetheless, Stafford was charged with "conduct to the prejudice of good order and military discipline," found guilty, and dismissed from the service.[5]

3. Stafford quarreled frequently with officers in white units who he believed were treating his men unfairly. One such incident took place on December 2, 1862, at Camp Stevens near Thibodaux when Stafford, apparently under the influence of liquor, ran his horse over Captain Richard Barrett while Barrett was drilling Company B of the 1st Louisiana Cavalry (Charges and Specifications preferred against Col. S. H. Stafford of the first regiment of Louisiana Native Guards, in Stafford's Compiled Military Service Record, NA). In "Negro Troops in Blue and Gray" (p. 180), Berry confused this incident with the one on May 13 and treated the two as one. In addition, she misidentified the white unit in question as the 13th Louisiana Cavalry, possibly by reading the letter "B" of Company B as "13."

4. Captain J. P. Garland to Colonel E. P. Chapin, May 14, 1863, in Stafford's Compiled Military Service Record, NA.

5. Stafford to Banks, June 4, 1863, and Stafford to Major G. B. Halstead, May 19, 1863,

The incident occurred just days before the 1st and 3rd Regiments of the Native Guards received orders to join Banks's army at Port Hudson.[6] They reached Port Hudson on May 23 and two days later found themselves posted on the far right of the Union line facing a heavily fortified Confederate position on high bluffs overlooking the Mississippi River.[7] Lieutenant Colonel Bassett commanded the 1st Regiment following Stafford's arrest. Lieutenant Colonel Henry Finnegass assumed command of the 3rd after its colonel, John A. Nelson, was given overall command of both regiments.[8] The black troops were in great spirits.[9] At last they were going to get the chance to prove themselves in battle.

On Tuesday, May 26, General Banks ordered an all-out assault on the Confederate works for the next day. The Native Guards' position straddled the Telegraph Road that ran along the Mississippi River between Port Hudson and Bayou Sara near St. Francisville. Across the front of their position lay Big Sandy Creek.[10] The Confederates had burned a bridge spanning the stream, but Federal engineers had constructed a light footbridge to take its place. A detachment from the Native Guards crossed the footbridge on Tuesday afternoon and pushed Rebel skirmishers back toward the Confederate lines so that troops from the 42nd Massachusetts Infantry could throw a pontoon bridge across the marshy bog. Despite an occasional shell from Confederate batteries mounted on the bluffs of Port Hudson less than half

---

both in Stafford's Compiled Military Service Record, NA. General George L. Andrews recommended Stafford's dismissal on August 12, 1863. After the war, Stafford successfully appealed his case and was honorably discharged retroactive to the date of the original dismissal (Special Orders No. 1 [extract], January 3, 1871, AGO, War Department, copy in Stafford's Compiled Military Service Record, NA).

6. Special Orders No. 122, May 21, 1863, *OR,* Vol. XXVI, pt. 1, p. 498.

7. Irwin, *Nineteenth Army Corps,* 166; Wilson, *Black Phalanx,* 525.

8. George W. Williams, *A History of the Negro Troops in the War of the Rebellion, 1861–1865* (New York, 1888), 216. Finnegass had been a first lieutenant in the 9th Connecticut Infantry and transferred to the 3rd Regiment of the Native Guards on January 1, 1863 (*Official Army Register,* I, 274).

9. William H. Root, "The Experiences of a Federal Soldier in Louisiana in 1863," ed. L. Carroll Root, *Louisiana Historical Quarterly,* XIX (1936), 658.

10. The Big Sandy Creek was sometimes called Foster's Creek from the point of its confluence with the Little Sandy and the Mississippi River and is thus marked on some maps (David C. Edmonds, *The Guns of Port Hudson,* Vol. 2, *The Investment, Siege and Reduction* [Lafayette, La., 1984], 401, n. 4).

a mile away, work progressed, and the 280-foot span was completed by nightfall.[11]

The Union general in charge of the Native Guards was Brigadier General William Dwight, Jr. Dwight was thirty-one years old, the son of a Massachusetts family whose ancestors had arrived in America in 1635. Dwight had entered West Point in 1849 but had been allowed to resign just before graduation because of academic problems. It was rumored that he had been expelled "on account of his drunkenness and shameless association with obscene women." Dwight went into business following his resignation and pursued manufacturing interests until the Civil War, at which time he accepted the commission of lieutenant colonel in the 70th New York Infantry. Wounded during the Peninsula Campaign, Dwight was left for dead on the field of battle, captured, and eventually exchanged. Somewhat of a hero after his release, the pugnacious New Englander was given a brigadier's star and sent to Louisiana.[12]

Dwight's assignment at Port Hudson on the far right of the Union position was inconsequential given the plan of attack, but he saw in Banks's order an opportunity "to test the negro question," as Dwight put it. "I have had the negro Regts longest in the service assigned to me," he wrote to his mother on Tuesday evening, "and I am going to storm a detached work with them. You may look for hard fighting, or for a complete run away." Believing that this would be the first time black troops had been used in combat during the war, Dwight informed his mother that "the garrison will of course be incensed and fight defiantly. The negro will have the fate of his race on his conduct. I shall compromise nothing in making this attack," he added, "for I regard it as an experiment."[13]

Dwight prepared for the attack Wednesday morning by getting drunk before breakfast. He had not conducted a reconnaissance nor studied the maps; he knew nothing of the terrain over which the black troops would

11. Charles P. Bosson, *History of the Forty-second Regiment Infantry, Massachusetts Volunteers, 1862, 1863, 1864* (Boston, 1886), 364.

12. Warner, *Generals in Blue*, 134–35; Bacon, *Among the Cotton Thieves*, 158.

13. William Dwight, Jr., to his mother, May 26, 1863, in Dwight Family Papers, MAHS. Dwight's request that the two black regiments be assigned to him is confirmed by General Albert E. Paine in his diary on May 26, 1863, in William B. Stevens, *History of the Fiftieth Regiment of Infantry, Massachusetts Volunteer Militia, in the Late War of the Rebellion* (Boston, 1907), 144.

The Corps d'Afrique at Port Hudson. *Courtesy of the National Archives.*

Sketch of black line officers of the First Louisiana Native Guards from *Harper's Weekly.* They are (*left to right*): Capt. Charles Sentmanat, 2d Lieut. Victor Lavigne, 1st Lieut. Louis D. Lanien, 2d Lieut. Joseph L. Montieu, and Capt. Edgard C. Davis. *Courtesy of the Louisiana and Lower Mississippi Valley Collections, Louisiana State University Libraries.*

P. B. S. Pinchback. *Courtesy of the Library of Congress.*

Benjamin F. Butler (*courtesy of the Library of Congress*).

Nathaniel P. Banks (*courtesy of the National Archives*).

William Dwight, Jr. (*courtesy of MASS MOLLUS & USAMHI*).

George L. Andrews (*courtesy of MASS MOLLUS & USAMHI*).

Union commanders of the Native Guards

Two companies of the First Louisiana Native Guards disembarking at Fort McComb, Louisiana, as depicted in the February 28, 1863, issue of *Harper's Weekly. Courtesy of the Louisiana and Lower Mississippi Valley Collections, Louisiana State University Libraries.*

View of Ship Island, Mississippi, published in the February 8, 1862, issue of *Harper's Weekly. Courtesy of the Louisiana and Lower Mississippi Valley Collections, Louisiana State University Libraries.*

The Native Guards' approach to Port Hudson on May 27, 1863. Telegraph Road is in the upper left-hand corner of this photograph. The Native Guards charged across the road toward the entrenchments in the foreground on May 27. *Courtesy of the Illinois State Historical Society.*

Confederate earthworks at Port Hudson overlooking Telegraph Road. *Marshall Dunham Photograph Album, Louisiana and Lower Mississippi Valley Collections, LSU Libraries, Louisiana State University.*

Inaccurate depiction of the Native Guards' assault at Port Hudson published in *Frank Leslie's Illustrated Newspaper. Reprinted from* Leslie's Illustrated Civil War (*Jackson, Miss., 1992*), 202.

Sketch of Captain Cailloux's funeral procession in *Harper's Weekly,* August 29, 1863. *Courtesy of the Louisiana and Lower Mississippi Valley Collections, Louisiana State University Libraries.*

Interior view of a Union camp and fortifications at Port Hudson. *Courtesy of the National Archives.*

General Andrews' headquarters at Port Hudson (*courtesy of the National Archives*). "I send you a photograph of our headquarters," Colonel Quincy wrote in a letter home. "The first tent to the right [left?] is mine. You observe the General leaning against the fence. Lieut. Luther leaning against the tree. A sentinel on the pizarro [piazza?] which you may observe his white glove, but he is so black you cant see anything else. . . . The black man on the barrels a building of a chimney on Mr Fiske's tent. The next tent is Major Ward's, & the one on the extreme ~~right~~ left the General's. The house was occupied by the rebel general Gardner during the siege, & I am writing in the room of which you see the left hand window with the blinds. We find our tents much warmer in windy weather than the house, which is ventilated with our shells" (Col. Samuel M. Quincy to his mother, January 30, 1864, Quincy *et al.* Papers, LC).

School for black soldiers and freedmen at Port Hudson. *Photo by Blauvelt, ICHi-19841, courtesy of the Chicago Historical Society.*

Colonel Quincy standing on the porch, *second from the left,* listening to the band from Boston after its escape from New Orleans. *Courtesy of MASS MOLLUS & USAMHI.*

Colonel Dickey seated on a sleigh after an unusual snowfall at Port Hudson in January, 1864. *Courtesy of the Louisiana Office of State Parks.*

Black sentinel on a parapet at Port Hudson. *Courtesy of the National Archives.*

Corporal's Guard of black soliders in front of the Provost Marshall's Office at Port Hudson. *Courtesy of the National Archives.*

Black engineer troops working on entrenchments at Port Hudson. *Courtesy of the Illinois State Historical Society.*

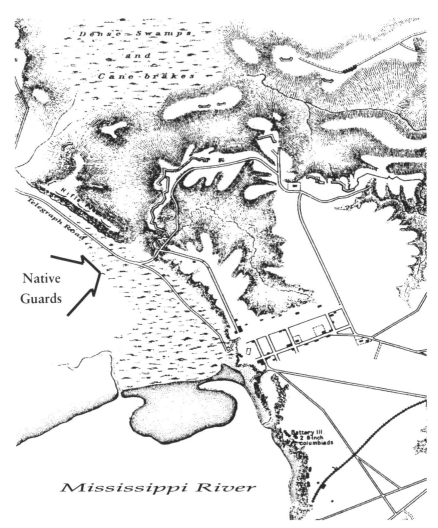

Map of the Native Guards' assault on Port Hudson. Adapted from Plate XXXVIII of *Atlas to Accompany the Official Records of the Union and Confederate Armies* (Washington, D.C., 1891–95).

advance. When Colonel Nelson asked what the ground would be like, Dwight lied. The approach would be "the easiest way into Port Hudson," he told Nelson. The ground to the front of the Native Guards was anything but easy. In fact, the rugged terrain and tangle of trees made the Confederate position the Native Guards were about to assault the strongest at Port Hudson.[14]

The main Confederate line was on a high bluff that dropped off abruptly to a floodplain adjacent to the Mississippi River. The river was high, and much of the floodplain was under water. Jutting out from the main position was a jagged finger of land on top of which the Confederates had dug a series of rifle pits. The position was about four hundred yards in length and ran parallel to Telegraph Road, along which the Native Guards would have to advance. The outwork was manned by a detachment of forty-five men from the 39th Mississippi Infantry and fifteen men from the 9th Louisiana Cavalry Battalion. The main Confederate position was held by six companies of the 39th Mississippi supported by two batteries containing a total of six fieldpieces. Because of the floodplain, the black troops would have little room to maneuver once they left the protection of the woods behind Union lines. To make matters worse, two eight-inch Columbiads in a water battery on the river could rake the road as the troops advanced.[15] The Native Guards would thus be exposed to fire from three sides: the Mississippians in the rifle pits on the high ground to their left, the cannon in the main works to their front, and the Columbiads in the water battery to their right.

Early Wednesday morning, six companies from the 1st Regiment and nine companies from the 3rd crossed the pontoon bridge over the Big Sandy and filed to the right to form a line of battle in a grove of willow trees that covered the old riverbed south of the Telegraph Road. Initially, they were supported by two brass guns from the 6th Massachusetts Artillery and some dismounted troopers from the 1st Louisiana Union Cavalry.[16] The artillerymen unlimbered in the road and engaged the Rebel guns on the bluffs ahead.

14. Bacon, *Among the Cotton Thieves*, 159–60; Lawrence Lee Hewitt, *Port Hudson, Confederate Bastion on the Mississippi* (Baton Rouge, 1987), 148.

15. Edward Cunningham, *The Port Hudson Campaign, 1862–1863* (Baton Rouge, 1963), 53; M. J. Smith and James Freret, "Fortification and Siege of Port Hudson," *Southern Historical Society Papers*, XIV (1886), 321–22; Hewitt, *Port Hudson*, 148; Irwin, *Nineteenth Army Corps*, 173.

16. Hewitt, *Port Hudson*, 148.

They fired only one round, however, before the Confederate artillery responded with a vengeance. Two artillerymen went down in the fusillade, and three horses were killed. Quickly, the boys from Massachusetts limbered their cannon and withdrew, leaving the Native Guards to fend for themselves.[17]

At about ten o'clock, the Native Guards left the relative protection of the willow trees and started forward at a double-quick.[18] About six hundred yards separated the black soldiers from the main Confederate position. They covered about two hundred yards before all hell broke loose. As a newspaper reported described it, the artillery opened fire with "shot and shells, and pieces of railroad iron twelve to eighteen inches long." The Mississippians in the rifle pits along the top of the outwork as well as infantry behind the breastworks commenced firing as soon as the black troops came within range.[19]

The color sergeant of the 1st Regiment, Anselmas Planciancois, was hit almost immediately, a shell taking off half of his head and splattering his brains on the men standing closest to him.[20] Two corporals on either side seized the colors before they hit the ground and tugged at the flagstaff between them, each wanting the honor of carrying it forward.[21] Captain Andre Cailloux was out in front of his company, urging the men on. His left arm

17. Bosson, *Forty-second Massachusetts*, 364; Smith and Freret, "Fortification and Siege of Port Hudson," 321. Smith and Freret reprinted a large portion of Colonel Shelby's after-action report to Gardner (dated August 5, 1863, and addressed to Major S. F. Wilson, Gardner's AAG), which Shelby wrote from prison in New Orleans. The original is in the Louisiana Historical Association Collection, 55-B, Box 8, folder 5, HTML. Also see Lieutenant Fred M. Dabney's report on the siege of Port Hudson dated August 24, 1863, and found in the same folder as Shelby's report.

18. Although the exact time the Native Guards began their assault is uncertain, it is known that they began to advance after Weitzel's attack had ended but before Augur's began (John C. Palfrey, "Port Hudson," in *The Mississippi Valley, Tennessee, Georgia, Alabama, 1861–1864*, vol. 8, *Papers of the Military Historical Society of Massachusetts* [Boston, 1910], 41). Banks placed their advance in conjunction with Weitzel's at 10 A.M. (Banks to Halleck, May 30, 1863, *OR*, Vol. XXVI, Pt. 1, pp. 43–44).

19. Smith and Freret, "Fortification and Siege of Port Hudson," 322; Chicago *Daily Tribune*, June 10, 1863.

20. Joseph E. Roy, "Our Indebtedness to the Negroes for Their Conduct During the War," *New Englander and Yale Review*, LI (1889), 358; Williams, *History of Negro Troops*, 217.

21. Wilson, *Black Phalanx*, 214.

dangled uselessly by his side; a ball had shattered his elbow.[22] The Native Guards followed Cailloux across the open ground, only to see him cut down in a torrent of shot and shell.[23] Cailloux's death and the deadly fire from the Confederate position were too much for the Native Guards. After firing a single volley, they fell back in confusion.[24]

The Confederates continued to fire at the retreating troops. "We moad them down," one Louisiana artillerist recalled, "and made them disperse[,] leaving there dead and wounded on the field to stink."[25] A small contingent of black soldiers found that they could not retreat and hugged the ground under the lip of the hill between the Confederate rifle pits and the river. Although they were shielded from direct fire from the rifle pits above, these men were easy targets for the eight-inch Columbiads in the water battery.[26] Scarcely fifteen minutes had passed since the Native Guards had begun their assault. Although they left scores of dead and wounded behind them, the Native Guards had not inflicted a single casualty on the Confederate defenders.[27]

Nelson sent an aide to Dwight, informing the general of the failed assault and asking for orders. The aide found Dwight seated on the ground leaning against a tree. "Tell Colonel Nelson," Dwight told the aide, "I shall consider he has done nothing unless he carries the enemy's works."[28] The aide protested, pointing out that both regiments had been cut up badly and had lost half their men. "Charge again," Dwight commanded, "and let the impetuosity of the charge counterbalance the paucity of numbers." Apparently, Dwight was determined to press his experiment to its deadly conclusion.[29]

22. Brown, *The Negro in the American Rebellion,* 169, 171.

23. New York *Times,* June 13, 1863.

24. Hewitt, *Port Hudson,* 148–49; Irwin, *Nineteenth Army Corps,* 174; J. V. Frederick, ed., "War Diary of W. C. Porter," *Arkansas Historical Quarterly,* XI (1952), 313–14. An account in Wilson's *Black Phalanx* (pp. 525–26) alleges that Captain Quinn and thirty-five or forty men actually breached the backwater and scaled the Rebel parapets. This account also claims that the Native Guards made six separate assaults. There is no evidence from other sources to indicate that this account is accurate.

25. Undated notes in Robert Hughes Papers, United States Military History Institute, Carlisle Barracks, Pa.

26. Frederick, ed., "War Diary of Porter," 313–14.

27. Smith and Freret, "Fortification and Siege of Port Hudson," 322.

28. Johns, *Life with the Forty-ninth Massachusetts Volunteers,* 254–55.

29. Stanyan, *Eighth New Hampshire Volunteers,* 229–30. Dwight's language was so bi-

The aide recrossed the creek and relayed Dwight's orders. Nelson sent word to Bassett and Finnegass to prepare the men for another assault. But rather than start his men forward, Finnegass retreated to Nelson's command post behind the lines and asked the colonel for a chew of tobacco. Nelson ordered Finnegass to return to his regiment. Finnegass started back to the front, only to show up again a few minutes later. This time he wanted a drink of whiskey. And would the colonel have a match so he could light his pipe? Valuable time was being wasted. Return to your men and lead the advance, Nelson told the reluctant lieutenant colonel. It would be of no use to advance, Finnegass replied; the Rebel position was far too strong. Could he take his men to the rear to reform them? Nelson was flabbergasted. No, he said. A withdrawal under these conditions would demoralize the troops and encourage the Confederates on bluffs waiting for the attack. Finnegass said he would be damned if he would go and stood off to the side as if that settled the matter.[30]

Finnegass' refusal to obey orders, the strength of the Confederate position, and the heavy casualties already sustained made it clear to Nelson that it would be suicidal for the Native Guards to charge again. He also realized that the drunken Dwight had no intention of leaving the safety of his headquarters to see whether his order was being obeyed. Consequently, Nelson ordered the men to continue firing from their position among the willows. Although they would not be able to hit any Confederates from there, at least they were not out in the open, and the sound of firing would make Dwight believe that his insane order was being carried out.

Throughout the afternoon, the Native Guards continued to shoot at the distant enemy. They were safe from rifle fire, but the Confederate guns shelled the thicket, shattering limbs and sending splinters from the frag-

zarre that Stanyan took pains in his memoirs to assure the reader that the quotation was accurate. Also see the New York *Times,* June 13, 1863; Bacon, *Among the Cotton Thieves,* 159–61; Irwin, *Nineteenth Army Corps,* 174; Smith and Freret, "Fortification and Siege of Port Hudson," 321–22.

30. John A. Nelson to Captain Dunham, June 1, 1863, and Charges and Specifications preferred against Lieut. Col. Henry Finnegass, 3rd Regt, Corps d'Afrique (no date), both in Finnegass' Compiled Military Record, NA. Finnegass was also absent from his regiment later that night when a false alarm caused the Native Guards to fall in under arms to repel a Confederate cavalry charge that did not materialize.

mented trees slicing through the air.[31] Casualties would have been higher except that the Rebel gunners could not depress their guns sufficiently to do further damage.[32] Nevertheless, the wounded continued to stream to the rear. One man, his arm shattered by a shell, walked along using his good arm to swing the broken one like a plumb weight. "Massa, guess I can't fight no more," he commented to an officer. Another wounded black soldier refused to leave the field. "I been shot bad in de leg, Captain, and dey want me to go to de hospital, but I guess I can gib 'em some more yet." He then propped himself on a log and "Sat With his leg a swinging and bleeding and fierd thirty rounds of Ammunition" before allowing himself to be taken to the field hospital. He died a few days later.[33]

The Native Guards were not the only soldiers in Banks's army to be repulsed that day. Every charge in every sector failed. The firing continued sporadically until 5:30 that evening, when someone had the good sense to raise a white flag and call a temporary cease-fire so that the wounded could be attended to. Union casualties on May 27 exceeded 450 dead and missing and over 1,500 wounded. Confederate losses numbered no more than several hundred.[34]

The Native Guards had gone into battle with fewer than 540 men in each regiment.[35] The 1st Regiment had lost two officers. One was Captain André Cailloux. The other was Second Lieutenant John H. Crowder, the young steamboat steward who had attempted to defend a lady's honor. Twenty-

31. Hewitt, *Port Hudson,* 150, 149.

32. Bosson, *Forty-Second Massachusetts,* 365.

33. New York *Times,* June 13, 1863; George R. Sanders to Mr. Burnham, July 15, 1863, in Civil War Miscellaneous Collection, YU. There are two accounts of this incident, which may refer to two different men or be two versions of the same event. I have chosen to treat them as two versions of the same event.

34. Edmonds, *The Guns of Port Hudson,* II, 93; Banks to Halleck, June 29, 1863, *OR,* Vol. XXVI, Pt. 1, p. 47, also pp. 144, 147.

35. The figure of 1,080 men in both regiments combined comes from the New York *Times,* June 13, 1863. Where the correspondent got his numbers is unknown, but it is the best estimate we have. The Union report of troop strength in *OR,* Vol. XXVI, Pt. 1, p. 526, dated May 31, 1863, combines the 1st and 3rd Regiments with the 4th, which did not participate in the assault of May 27, for a total of 2,252 men present for duty. The 4th Regiment, which had been recruited just two months earlier, was probably somewhat larger than the 1st and 3rd. In addition, only six companies of the 1st and nine of the 3rd participated in the assault.

four enlisted men were also killed in action. Three officers and ninety-two men in the 1st Regiment were wounded. The 3rd Regiment lost a total of ten killed and thirty-eight wounded.[36]

Statistics alone belied the punishment these men had suffered. Captain Thomas C. Prescott of the 8th New Hampshire Infantry appreciated how much the black soldiers had sacrificed when his company marched down Telegraph Road later that evening. "They suffered severe losses," he wrote, "and as we moved back at night to our quarters, we passed the little house on the road where a temporary hospital had been established for them, and at the back door of this house we saw a pile of considerable size of legs and arms which had been amputated from those poor fellows."[37]

36. *OR,* Vol. XXVI, Pt. 1, p. 68. Two of the dead in the 1st Regiment, Louis Laville and Louis Fernandez, had served in the Louisiana militia.
37. Stanyan, *Eighth New Hampshire,* 230.

6

THE EQUAL OF ANY
"YANKEE TROOPS"
YOU WILL FIND

During the truce on the evening of
May 27, Union medics and hospital orderlies scurried about the battlefield,
retrieving the wounded and burying the dead under the watchful eyes of
hardened Confederates lounging on the top of their parapet. This activity
proceeded in all sectors except along Telegraph Road, where the Native
Guards had launched their attack. For some reason, the flag of truce did not
make an appearance there, leaving the black dead to lie where they had
fallen.[1] In the days that followed, their bodies swelled and putrefied in the
hot summer sun. Among them was Captain André Cailloux, whose corpse
was closer to the Confederate works than to the Union lines. The Native
Guards made several attempts to retrieve his remains, but Rebel sharpshooters kept them at bay.[2] Finally, the stench became so unbearable that Colonel
W. B. Shelby of the 39th Mississippi sent a message through the lines, asking
Banks to allow his men to bury the black dead. When he received Shelby's

1. "Siege of Port Hudson," New Orleans *Times Democrat,* April 26, 1906, Sec. 2, p. 8;
Wilson, *Black Phalanx,* 214; Donald E. Everett, "Free Persons of Color in New Orleans, 1803–
1865" (Ph.D. dissertation, Tulane University, 1952), 315.
2. New York *Times,* August 8, 1863.

message, Banks is reputed to have said that there were no Union dead in that sector.[3]

Both sides continued to strengthen their positions at Port Hudson. Surrounded, the Confederate troops could do little more than burrow deeper into the bluffs and ravines around the little village. Meanwhile, Banks received reinforcements, more than enough to make up for the losses of May 27.[4] By June 13 Banks was ready for another grand assault. After a fierce artillery bombardment, Banks sent the Confederate commander, Major General Franklin K. Gardner, a message demanding immediate surrender. Gardner laughed out loud when he read it. No, he would not surrender.[5] Banks ordered an attack for the next day.

The Native Guards were held in reserve on June 14.[6] Two companies from the 1st Regiment captured the detached rifle pits that had defied them two weeks earlier, but otherwise the black troops were idle.[7] They were lucky, for the second assault was as disastrous as the first. Union regiments were pinned down by a murderous fire everywhere. "How do you like it?"

3. Edward Young McMorries, *History of the First Regiment, Alabama Volunteer Infantry, C.S.A.*, Publication of the State of Alabama Department of Archives and History, no. 2 (Montgomery, 1904), 64–65.

4. Hewitt, *Port Hudson,* 170–71.

5. Crawford M. Jackson, "An Account of the Occupation of Fort Hudson," *Alabama Historical Quarterly,* XVIII (1956), 475.

6. A diary entry for June 13, 1863, in James F. Dargan, *My Experiences in Service, or a Nine Months Man,* American Classics Facsimile Series, ed. Norman Tanis (Los Angeles, 1974), Book 3, confirms the Native Guards' status as a reserve on June 14. Dargan defended the decision not to use black troops in the assault "as the 27th of May demonstrated they cannot stand the fire like the white troops."

7. General Affidavit in pension file for James Lewis, NA; see also "Will the Negro Fight?" New Orleans *L'Union,* July 14, 1863. Berry ("Negro Troops in Blue and Gray," 188) and Brown (*The Negro in the American Rebellion,* 174–75) give the impression that the Native Guards were actively engaged in the assault of June 14. McConnell ("Louisiana's Black Military History," 56) reinforces this notion, citing company muster rolls for the months of May and June, 1863. Muster rolls generally do not indicate the date on which deaths occurred (i.e., whether on May 27 or June 14). But the monthly morning report for the "1st Louisiana Vols. Native Guard" dated June 2, 1863, twelve days before the second assault, accounts for all twenty-six men from this regiment who lost their lives at Port Hudson. In addition, a letter dated July 15, 1863, from a hospital steward in the 3rd Regiment, describes the casualties resulting from the May 27 assault but says nothing about the Native Guards taking part in the attack of June 14 (Sanders to Burnham, in Civil War Miscellaneous Collection, YU).

a Rebel with a boyish voice taunted as the Union troops huddled behind tree stumps and in ravines. "Why don't you come on?" another Confederate called out in a rough voice from behind the parapet. The failed assault on June 14 resulted in another four hundred dead and missing and fourteen hundred wounded. The attacks of May 27 and June 14 combined had resulted in more than four thousand Union casualties, or one man in five.[8]

Banks refused to give up and called for a thousand men to form a special storming party "to vindicate the flag of the Union and the memory of the defenders who have fallen." Banks named them the "Forlorn Hope" and promised recognition, promotion, and a medal to those who volunteered. More than thirteen hundred men came forward, among them fifty-four volunteers from the 1st Regiment of the Native Guards and thirty-seven from the 3rd. Only two white regiments (the 13th Connecticut and the 14th Maine) offered more volunteers than either regiment of the Native Guards. By comparison, five of the eight regiments from Massachusetts, Banks's home state, responded with only one or two volunteers from each. Nevertheless, Banks was unimpressed by the Native Guards' patriotic display and refused to accept them as part of his elite force.[9] The all-white Forlorn Hope never got its chance for glory, however, for Port Hudson was a sideshow to the big show up the river at Vicksburg, and Gardner surrendered the Port Hudson garrison five days after that citadel fell to Grant on July 4.

After the capitulation ceremony on July 9, Federal troops occupied the Confederate works they had tried so hard to capture. The Native Guards climbed the steep bluff beside the Mississippi River and entered Shelby's position to stand guard over the men who had tried to kill them six weeks before. A colonel from the 6th Michigan Infantry came across the black Union soldiers and their white Confederate prisoners as he completed a walking tour of the Rebel positions. "Proud old Southerners and their fiery sons, wild Texans and tawny Creoles, are here," he wrote, describing the prisoners. "Some of them, perhaps, recognize their own waiters or field hands among the sentinels who march leisurely to and fro, clad in federal blue, and carrying Springfield muskets. But what an exhibition of human nature," the colonel thought to himself. "The rebels, one and all, appear to

8. Bacon, *Among the Cotton Thieves,* 178; *OR,* Vol. XXVI, Pt. 1, pp. 67–72.

9. Irwin, *Nineteenth Army Corps,* 212–13, 488–506. Eight of the volunteers for the Forlorn Hope from the 1st Regiment had served in the Louisiana militia.

be enjoying a comfortable rest, and are talking to the negroes with a familiarity which would shock Northern volunteers." Such was the curious and contradictory relationship between blacks and whites in the American South.[10]

The Native Guards had fought well at Port Hudson, given their inexperience and the strength of the position Dwight had ordered them to take. In his official report, Banks noted that their conduct on May 27 "in many respects . . . was heroic. They require only good officers . . . and careful discipline to make them excellent soldiers." In a letter to his wife three days after the assault, Banks wrote: "They fought splendidly!, splendidly! Every body is delighted that they did so well! Their charges upon the rebel works, of which they made three, exhibited the greatest bravery and caused them to suffer great losses."[11] Banks's assessment was too favorable given what the Native Guards had actually accomplished, but his comments reflected the most important aspect of their assault that day. Black troops had gone head-to-head with the Rebels and had not run away.[12]

The word spread quickly through Banks's army. "The negroes are fighting bravely, and have triumphantly vindicated themselves from the aspersions cast upon their courage," one soldier wrote in his diary. Another recorded that "all accounts are [that] the Negro fought well, bravely begging their chance to lead the charge." Even the skeptical Colonel Paine of the 2nd Louisiana was forced to admit that "the darkies fought well."[13]

10. Bacon, *Among the Cotton Thieves,* 288–89. For a discussion of this relationship, see Joel Williamson, *The Crucible of Race: Black-White Relations in the American South Since Emancipation* (New York, 1984), 11–43.

11. Banks to Halleck, May 30, 1863, *OR,* Vol. XXVI, Pt. 1, pp. 44–45, also in the *National Intelligencer,* June 10, 1863; Banks to Mary Banks, May 30, 1863, in Nathaniel P. Banks Collection, LC. The number of assaults made by the Native Guards on May 27 is a matter of debate. Banks and others (e.g., Benjamin Quarles, *The Negro in the Civil War* [Boston, 1953], 218) thought three, others said six. Hewitt (*Port Hudson,* 150) discounts reports of multiple assaults, as do I.

12. Frank M. Flinn, *Campaigning with Banks in Louisiana, '63 and '64, and with Sheridan in the Shenandoah Valley in '64 and '65* (Lynn, Mass., 1887), 74; George H. Hepworth, *The Whip, Hoe and Sword; or, The Gulf-Department in '63* (Boston, 1864), 187–90; Johns, *Life with the Forty-ninth Massachusetts Volunteers,* 254–57; and Moors, *History of the Fifty-second Massachusetts Volunteers,* 159–60.

13. Entry for June 13, 1863, in Lorin L. Dame Diary, May 30, 1863, in Civil War Corre-

Reports of the Native Guards' assault that reached the North often bore little resemblance to what had actually happened.[14] Some accounts contained major errors. "Col. Daniel's Second Louisiana negro regiment distinguished itself," the Boston *Daily Evening Transcript* reported, "especially in charging upon the enemy's siege guns, losing killed and wounded over 600." Other newspaper reports overestimated the success of the black troops' attack. "I should be guilty of inexcusable reticence did I fail to chronicle the gallantry of two Louisiana colored regiments—the First, Col. Stafford, and the Second [*sic*], Col. Nelson," a reporter for the Chicago *Daily Tribune* told his readers. "A New Orleans Copperhead informed me that they fought like Tigers," he continued. "Six times did they charge upon the fortifications, clambering over a huge abatis and marching unitedly forward, while at each step the concentrated fire of the adjacent batteries lessened their ranks with fearful rapidity. Fairly fifty percent of their number were left dead upon the bush-heaps to demonstrate their bravery."[15]

---

spondence, Diaries and Journals, roll 10, MAHS; Entry for May 30, 1863, in James Miller Diary, *ibid.*, roll 11; Charles J. Paine to his father, June 25, 1863, in Paine Letters (microfilm P-382), MAHS. General Dwight failed to tell his mother how his experiment turned out. "I am very well and very tired," he wrote shortly after the battle. "We had a bad go off on the 27th, but I did good" (Dwight to his mother, May 30, 1863, in Dwight Family Papers, MAHS). Paine's admission of black bravery was the beginning of a gradual transformation of his attitude toward the use of black troops. A year later in Virginia, while a member of Benjamin F. Butler's staff, Paine reported after an assult on the Confederate lines at Petersburg that "the darkies did splendidly" (Paine to his father, June 17, 1864, original in possession of Thomas M. Paine, Wellesley, Mass.). By the end of the war, at which time he commanded a black division, Paine had ceased using the term *darkies* and referred to black troops as "colored soldiers" or simply "my men" (e.g., Paine to his father, April 15, September 8, 1865, both in possession of Thomas M. Paine).

14. Kenneth Shewmaker and Andrew Prinz, eds., "A Yankee in Louisiana: Selections from the Diary and Correspondence of Henry R. Gardner, 1862–1866," *Louisiana History,* V (1964), 277; Willoughby M. Babcock, Jr., ed., *Selections from the Letters and Diaries of Brevet-Brigadier General Willoughby Babcock of the Seventy-fifth New York Volunteers* (Albany, 1922), 80. For exaggerations, see Flinn, *Campaigning with Banks in Louisiana*, 74, Hepworth, *The Whip, Hoe and Sword*, 187–90, and Johns, *Life with the Forty-ninth Massachusetts Volunteers,* 254–57.

15. Boston *Daily Evening Transcript*, June 6, 1863. Colonel Daniels' regiment was still on Ship Island in the Gulf of Mexico. Chicago *Daily Tribune,* June 11, 1863. Colonel Nelson apparently contributed to the inaccuracy of these accounts by enlarging the number of charges

These newspaper accounts were often accepted at face value by combat-
ants who had been at Port Hudson but who had not witnessed the Native
Guards' assault firsthand.[16] For example, the quartermaster's clerk of the
49th Massachusetts Infantry, in his widely read memoirs published in 1864,
dutifully recorded that the Native Guards had assaulted the Rebel works six
times:

> All agree that none fought more boldly than the "native guards." They drove the
> rebels from their outer works, and against them, *behind* their formidable en-
> trenchments, made *six* charges. *Six* times they repeated *our* charge. True, they
> had to advance but two hundred yards under fire, while twelve hundred yards
> lay between us [the 49th Massachusetts Infantry] and the foe, but *six* times did
> they go over the ground, heaping it with their slain, and pressed into the ditch,
> over which a few gallantly passed, and mounted the ramparts of the foe.[17]

As the stories of the Native Guards' assault of May 27 were repeated
throughout the North, some accounts became wildly exaggerated.[18] An il-
lustration in *Frank Leslie's Illustrated Newspaper* depicted a black soldier
of large stature planting the Stars and Stripes on top of the Confederate
ramparts while a seedy-looking Rebel prepared to stick him with a bayonet.
Other accounts became ridiculous through exaggeration. "One negro was
observed with a rebel soldier in his grasp, tearing the flesh from his face with
his teeth, other weapons having failed him," a correspondent reported. "After firing one volley they did not deign to load again, but went in with
bayonets, and whenever they had a chance it was all up with the rebels."[19]

---

and exaggerating the extent of the casualties suffered by the Native Guards (Willoughby Babcock, "War Commentary," 28, in vol. 9 of the Willoughby Babcock and Family Papers,
MNHS).

16. These accounts, in turn, have been perpetuated in more recent studies of the Native
Guards (*e.g.*, McConnell, "Louisiana's Black Military History," 52–54).

17. Johns, *Life with the Forty-ninth Massachusetts Volunteers*, 254–55.

18. For example, Moors, *History of the Fifty-second Massachusetts Volunteers*, 159–60,
191. Exaggerated accounts also appeared in Southern newspapers sympathetic toward black
soldiers (*e.g.*, "Charge of the Black Regiment at Port Hudson," New Orleans *Black Republican*,
May 13, 1865).

19. *Leslie's Illustrated Civil War* (1894; rpr. Jackson: University Press of Mississippi, 1992),
202; unidentified correspondent quoted in John Robertson, *Michigan in the War* (Lansing,
Mich., 1882), 267.

By comparison, reports of the Native Guards' assault from the Confederate side tended to derogate their bravery. "They broke at our fire and clustered behind willow trees apparently too panic-stricken either to advance or run," a Confederate lieutenant recorded. "On account of white troops behind them they probably had some difficulty getting away," he asserted, "but in fifteen minutes after they first appeared none of them were to be seen except the dead and those too badly wounded to crawl off." An Alabamian manning one of the guns in the main Confederate line claimed later that once the Confederates opened fire they "turned and fled, without firing a shot." Reports in the Rebel press also claimed that the black troops had been forced to charge at gunpoint and had held their ground only because white troops behind them prevented a headlong flight to the rear. About the only thing Southern and Northern accounts could agree on was the futility of the assault. "If there is any glory in being thus substituted for breastworks and being sacrificed for the protection of others," the Charleston *Mercury* reported, "the negros have covered themselves all over with that dear-bought commodity." [20]

Confederate attempts to disparage the conduct of the Native Guards at Port Hudson were to be expected. Evidence of black bravery under fire would seriously challenge the assumptions upon which the institution of slavery was based. As Confederate General Howell Cobb noted during the closing months of the war, when Richmond was debating the possibility of arming slaves for service in the Confederate army, "Use all the Negroes you can get for all purposes for which you need them[,] but don't arm them. The day you make soldiers of them is the beginning of the end of the [Southern] revolution. If slaves make good soldiers, our whole theory of slavery is wrong." [21]

The truth regarding the Native Guards' assault at Port Hudson is probably somewhere between the Northern and Southern accounts. They had charged once, held their ground briefly, and then retreated under tremendous

20. Howard C. Wright, *Port Hudson: Its History from an Interior Point of View as Sketched from the Diary of an Officer* (1937; rpr. Baton Rouge, 1961), 36, originally printed in the New Orleans *Daily True Delta*, August 9, 1863; Daniel P. Smith, *Company K, First Alabama Regiment: or, Three Years in the Confederate Service* (N.d., rpr. Gaithersburg, Mo., 1984), 63; "How the Yankees Drove the Negros to Slaughter at Port Hudson," Charleston *Mercury,* August 14, 1863.
21. Howell Cobb to James A. Seddon, January 8, 1865, *OR*, Ser. IV, Vol. III, p. 1009.

fire. "From a comparison of all accounts," a Union colonel wrote after the war, "it is clear that the negroes behaved with considerable courage, but that they were handled most cruelly."[22]

The Native Guards' assault was the first major encounter of black troops with the Confederate army on the battlefield.[23] Although it was a tactical defeat, it became a strategic victory with profound implications.[24] Because of the widespread, if exaggerated, praise of their bravery in the North, efforts to enlist blacks in the Union army redoubled.[25]

Official sanction for enlisting black troops predated the assault at Port Hudson by several months. In fact, Banks had begun to add to Butler's Native Guards almost as soon as he arrived in New Orleans.[26] In addition, the administration had come to embrace the recruitment of black troops after Lincoln signed the Emancipation Proclamation on January 1, 1863. Despite his earlier doubts, Lincoln had come to see former slaves as "the great available, yet unavailed of, force for restoring the Union." To emphasize the point, in January, 1863, he had ordered Brigadier General Daniel Ullmann to the Department of the Gulf with two hundred officers recruited from the Army of the Potomac and authority to raise a black brigade. Two months later, Lincoln sent Brigadier General Lorenzo Thomas to Grant's

22. Babcock, "War Commentary," 29, MNHS.

23. There had been a handful of skirmishes involving black soldiers in Kansas, Florida, and Mississippi (*i.e.*, the 2nd Regiment's foray to East Pascagoula), but they were not of sufficient magnitude or intensity to address the question of whether black troops would stand and fight (Glatthaar, *Forged in Battle,* 123).

24. Berry, "Negro Troops in Blue and Gray," 189–90; Hewitt, *Port Hudson,* 174–79; Williams, *History of Negro Troops,* 221.

25. Glatthaar, *Forged in Battle,* 32, 141–42. A hard-fought battle at Milliken's Bend on June 7, 1863, which involved the first hand-to-hand combat between black Union troops and Confederate soldiers during the Civil War, and the celebrated assault of the 54th Massachusetts Infantry (Colored) on Fort Wagner five weeks later also contributed to a change in attitudes that helped accelerate the recruitment of black soldiers.

26. Banks to Halleck, December 17, 1863, *OR,* Vol. XXVI, Pt. 1, p. 457. The 4th Louisiana Native Guards were mustered into the service on March 6, 1863 (*Official Army Register,* VIII, 252), and were the only other regiment to bear the "Native Guards" designation. Banks raised a black engineer regiment in April, 1863, but it was designated as the 1st Regiment of Louisiana Engineers (*OR,* Vol. XXVI, Pt. 1, p. 539). There were two, perhaps three, batteries of light artillery that may have been designated as Native Guards, but information on these units is sketchy (*e.g., OR,* Vol. XV, pp. 15, 713; Vol. XXVI, Pt. 1, p. 531; and *Official Army Register,* VIII, 157).

command in the Mississippi Valley to oversee the organization of black units there.[27]

The die had thus been cast by March, 1863, but public support for the use of black soldiers in the Union army was lacking.[28] Before the Native Guards' assault at Port Hudson, the Northern press was primarily concerned with whether their enlistment would strengthen Southern resistance and create discontent in the North. "The time is past when we could afford to carry out this war for the purpose of elucidating theory, or loosening an ethnological knot," read an editorial in the New York *Times* on January 9, 1863. The main question regarding the enlistment of black soldiers, the editorial continued, was "its immediate effects . . . on the fortunes of war."

The Native Guards' assault of May 27 at Port Hudson turned editorial caution into enthusiastic support. On June 11, 1863, the New York *Times* made it clear that the time for accepting blacks into the Union army had arrived.

This official testimony [Banks's report] settles the question that the negro race can fight with great prowess. Those black soldiers had never before been in any severe engagement. They were comparatively raw troops, and were yet subjected to the most awful ordeal that even veterans ever had to experience—the charging upon fortifications through the crash of belching batteries. The men, white or black, who will not flinch from that, will flinch from nothing. It is no longer possible to doubt the bravery and steadiness of the colored race, when rightly led.

Even after Port Hudson, not everyone was convinced that black soldiers would fight.[29] "You have heard doubtless a great deal about negro soldiers,"

27. Cornish, *Sable Arm,* 95; Lincoln to Andrew Johnson, March 26, 1863, *OR,* Ser. III, Vol. III, p. 103; Thos. M. Vincent to Ullmann, January 13, 1863, *OR,* Ser. III, Vol. III, p. 14; Williams, *History of Negro Troops,* 102; Stanton to Thomas, March 25, 1863, *OR,* Ser. III, Vol. III, pp. 100–103.

28. Cornish, *Sable Arm,* 96.

29. Curiously, an opposite but equally cynical attitude arose. "Before the assault of the 27th May last on this place [Port Hudson]," Ullmann wrote to a friend in New York, "their [pro-slavery Union generals'] ridicule of the idea that the blacks would fight was constant. They then swung to the other side—forsooth they fight too well. 'We must not discipline them,' for if we do, we will have to fight them some day ourselves. Above all we must keep artillery out

a white enlisted man from New Hampshire wrote his brother in August, 1863. "I am inclined to believe that they will make good soldiers, better in fact, in drill and discipline than whites, but as to whether they will fight as well remains yet a mooted question." For most, however, Port Hudson had settled the matter. A newspaper correspondent who had observed black troops in the Department of the Gulf for nearly a year concluded that in spite of his initial reservations, "at least two-thirds of the men slaves would make brave and effective soldiers." Freedmen "make excellent soldiers[,] learn very quick," a Massachusetts soldier wrote his sister. "At the recent fight at Port Hudson I have it from eye witnesses Troops never fought better." A soldier from Connecticut wrote a friend back home predicting confidently that black troops "will be the equal of any 'Yankee troops' you can find." [30]

The growing acceptance of black soldiers was reflected by the success with which they were recruited into the Union army. "One thing I am glad to say," a Union captain wrote his father on June 3, "is that the black troops at P. Hudson fought & acted superbly. The theory of negro inefficiency is, I am very thankful[,] at last thoroughly Exploded by facts. We shall shortly have a splendid army of thousands of them." [31] By August, 1863, Banks would have more than ten thousand in the Department of the Gulf alone. [32] Thomas would raise twice that number along the Mississippi River during the same period. By the end of the war, one man in ten in the United States Army would be black. [33]

---

of their hands" (Ullmann to William C. Bryant, March 7, 1864, in Woodward, comp., *The Negro in the Military Service of the United States*, 2412 [M-858, roll 3], NA).

30. John H. Guild to his brother, August 10, [1863], in Guild Letters, LALMVC; New York *Daily Tribune*, June 6, 1863; see also New York *Times*, March 9, 1863; Charles Bennett to "Friend Charley," May 14, 1863, in Charles Bennett Letters, HNOC; William H. Eastman to his sister, June 8, 1863, in William H. Eastman Letters, MAHS. Charles Paine reached a similar conclusion a year and a half later after he became the commander of a black division. "My div. has had severe fighting," he wrote from Virginia, "& no troops in U.S. Service ever did it better" (Charles J. Paine to his father, October 3, 1864, in Paine Letters (microfilm P-382), MAHS.

31. Captain Robert F. Wilkinson to his father, June 3, 1863, in Misc. Mss., R. F. Wilkinson, NYHS.

32. Banks to Lincoln, August 17, 1863, OR, Vol. XXVI, Pt. 1, pp. 688–89. More black troops were raised in Louisiana than in any other state (Gladstone, *United States Colored Troops*, 120).

33. Cornish, *Sable Arm*, 114, 288.

The great clamor that arose over the Native Guards' bravery at Port Hudson obviously was lost on those who fell in the futile charge of May 27. Among them was Captain André Cailloux, whose decomposed remains were finally recovered and brought to New Orleans for burial. His was a somber yet impressive funeral. The band of the 42nd Massachusetts Infantry played the usual dirges, while six black captains from the 2nd Regiment of Native Guards acted as pallbearers. Flowers were strewn around the flag-draped casket, and candles burned continuously. After receiving the last rites of the Catholic Church from a white priest, Cailloux's body was borne on the shoulders of eight black soldiers and placed in the hearse. Two companies of recruits for a new black regiment acted as the honor guard. About a hundred sick and convalescing soldiers from the Native Guards also were in attendance. Large crowds of civilians, both black and white, stood on the banquette along the Esplanade waiting for a chance to see the hearse as it passed. Eventually, the body reached the Bienville Street Cemetery, where Captain Cailloux, "the blackest man in New Orleans," was laid to rest.[34]

34. New York *Times*, August 8, 1863, reprinted in Wilson, *Black Phalanx*, 214, 216. Lieutenant Crowder's body was recovered after the assault of May 27 and returned to New Orleans, where it was buried in a pauper's grave (Glatthaar, "The Civil War Through the Eyes of a Sixteen-Year-Old Black Officer," 206).

7

UNSUITED FOR
THIS DUTY

After Port Hudson, Major General Nathaniel P. Banks moved aggressively to increase the number of black soldiers in the Department of the Gulf. Using the Native Guards as a nucleus, he set out to organize an entire division of black troops, the Corps d'Afrique, he called it. Accordingly, the 1st and 3rd Regiments of the Native Guards became the 1st and 3rd Regiments of the Corps d'Afrique and were placed under the command of Brigadier General Daniel Ullmann.[1] The 2nd Regiment on Ship Island became the 2nd Regiment of the Corps d'Afrique.[2]

During July and August, 1863, these soldiers joined white units clearing the countryside around Port Hudson of remaining Confederate resistance. A detachment from the 1st Regiment was on one of these missions when Confederate cavalry swept down near Jackson, Louisiana. The Rebels captured twenty-one black enlisted men and their black officer, Lieutenant Oscar

1. General Orders No. 40, May 1, 1863, *OR,* Vol. XV, pp. 716–17; also Vol. XXVI, Pt. 1, pp. 726, 733; Vol. LIII, p. 561; Irwin, *Nineteenth Army Corps,* 261. The change in designation from Native Guards to Corps d'Afrique was effective June 6, 1863 (General Orders No. 47, *OR,* Vol. XXVI, Pt. 1, p. 539).
2. Field and Staff Muster Roll, May and June, 1863, 74th U.S. Col'd Inf., in Compiled Military Service Records, NA.

Orillion.[3] The next morning, Colonel John L. Logan, the Rebel commander, ordered the 17th Arkansas Mounted Infantry to march the prisoners toward the Confederate lines. The guard set out several hours before the main body broke camp, took the wrong road, and eventually rejoined the main column minus the prisoners. Colonel John Griffith of the 17th Arkansas reported to Logan that four of the black soldiers had attempted to escape, which "created some excitement and a general stampede among them, all attempting to effect their escape." Colonel Frank Powers, Logan's cavalry commander, was more direct: "I ordered the guard to shoot them down. In the confusion, the other negroes attempted to escape likewise. I then ordered every one shot, and with my six shooter assisted in the execution of the order." Lieutenant James W. Shattuck of Scott's Louisiana Cavalry boasted later of having killed thirteen of the prisoners himself.[4]

The affair at Jackson gave evidence of the risk black men faced by serving in the Union army. This reality, coupled with their bravery before Port Hudson, should have increased the department commander's appreciation of their service. Instead, Banks chose to reward their loyalty in a very curious way; he decided to get rid of all the black officers who remained in the Corps d'Afrique. Black officers were a source of "constant embarrassment and annoyance," Banks wrote, and their use "demoralizes both the white troops and the negroes." Furthermore, Banks argued, the "arrogance and self-assertion" of the black officers caused white soldiers to retaliate with violence. As far as their being officers, Banks informed Lincoln in August, 1863, black men were simply "unsuited for this duty."[5]

In reality, it was the reaction of the white troops rather than the qualifications of the black officers that goaded Banks into taking action. Some of Banks's white troops threatened to go home if reenlisting meant that they had to salute a black man. As one lieutenant told a newspaper correspondent, if a black man were to be allowed to hold a commission, "I must not only obey him, I must politely touch my cap when I approach him. I must

3. George L. Andrews to Richard Irwin, August 6, 1863, OR, Vol. XXVI, Pt. 1, p. 239. Orillion's race can be deduced from the date of his commission, September 27, 1862, which made him one of the original officers of the 1st Regiment, Native Guards.

4. Frank Powers to John L. Logan, September 2, 1863, OR, Ser. II, Vol. VI, pp. 258–59, also pp. 244, 289, 960–61.

5. Banks to L. Thomas, February 12, 1863, OR, Ser. III, Vol. III, p. 46; New York Herald, February 4, 1863; Banks to Lincoln, August 16, 1863, OR, Vol. XXVI, Pt. 1, p. 689.

stand while he sits, unless his captainship should condescendingly ask me to be seated. Negro soldiers are all very well," he continued, "but let us have white officers, whom we can receive and treat as equals everywhere, and whom we may treat as superiors without humiliation." A provost marshal under Banks agreed. "You should have a look here at these negro Captains, appointed by Gen. Butler," he wrote to a friend shortly after arriving in New Orleans. To him they looked "like dogs in full dress, ready to dance in the menagerie. Would *you* like to obey such a fool?" he asked. Colonel Paine of the 2nd Louisiana put it more succinctly: "They ought never to put a shoulder strap on a darkey."[6]

Banks planned to replace all of the black officers by filling vacancies in the Corps d'Afrique with white men.[7] The mass resignation from the 3rd Regiment in February had aided him greatly in attaining this goal, but getting rid of the black officers in the 1st and 2nd Regiments would not be as easy. All of the line officers in both regiments were black, and their pride of serving in the first black regiments in the Union army was great. It did not take long, however, for Banks to formulate a strategy to force these men out of the service. First, he set up an examining board to evaluate the black officers' proficiency in military matters. Second, Banks let it be known that he intended to pay black enlisted men and their white field officers but not the black line officers.[8]

Banks's examining board was expected to apply the highest standards to the officers who came before it.[9] In practice, this meant black officers, for

6. Charles Bennett to his father, February 18, 1863, in Bennett Letters, HNOC; New York *Herald,* February 4, 1863; see also report of New York *Tribune* correspondent reprinted in Wilson, *Black Phalanx,* 527; Von Herrman to "My dear Captain," February 24, 1863, in Civil War Letters, 1862–63, Civil War Manuscripts Series, HTML; Charles J. Paine to his father, in Paine Letters (microfilm P-382), MAHS.

7. Banks to L. Thomas, February 12, 1863, *OR,* Ser. III, Vol. III, p. 46.

8. Captain P. B. S. Pinchback *et al.* to Banks, March 2, 1863, in Berlin *et al.,* eds., *Freedom,* Ser. II, 322. Banks did not follow through with his threat to withhold pay. The black officers were paid along with the men in early May, 1863 (John H. Crowder to his mother, May 4, 1863, in Glatthaar, "The Civil War Through the Eyes of a Sixteen-Year-Old Black Officer," 214).

9. New York *Times,* March 26, May 31, 1863; John W. Blassingame, "The Selection of Officers and Non-Commissioned Officers of Negro Troops in the Union Army, 1863–1865," *Negro History Bulletin,* XXX (1967), 8–12; Glatthaar, *Forged in Battle,* 35–59; Ripley, *Slaves and Freedmen in Civil War Louisiana,* 116–17.

their white counterparts were excused.[10] Three black officers from the 2nd Regiment were discharged from the service on February 24, 1863, for reasons of incompetence.[11] The other black officers on Ship Island reacted with anger and met on March 2 to formulate their grievances. Captain P. B. S. Pinchback served as their spokesman and offered a series of resolutions for the department commander's consideration. First, the officers complained that they were kept busy "continually erecting Batteries, Magazines, and Fortifications, working both day and night." This constant fatigue duty prevented them from preparing for the board examination. They also protested Banks's decision to withhold their pay. But the main problem was the examining board. Noting that white officers in the Corps d'Afrique did not have to pass an examination, the black officers charged that the examining board was a pretext for forcing them out of the service. "From the many rumors that have reached us," Pinchback wrote, "we are led to believe that it is the intention of the General to relieve us from our present command."[12]

Four of the petitioners anticipated Banks's reaction and did not wait for his reply. Ironically, all four had already been passed by the examining board.[13] The problem was prejudice. "When I joined the army I thought that I was fighting for the same cause, wishing only the success of my country would suffice to alter a prejudice which had long existed," Captain Arnold Bertonneau wrote in his letter of resignation from Fort Pike. "But I regret to say," he continued, "that five months experience has proved the contrary."

10. The War Department in Washington established examining boards for white officers in black regiments on May 22, 1863 (General Orders No. 144, in *OR*, Ser. III, Vol. III, p. 216), but the boards' standards for white officer candidates were described as "not to high" (Geo. B. Drake to Col. Sypher, October 2, 1864, in Woodward, comp., *The Negro in the Military Service of the United States*, 2796 [M-858, roll 3], NA). For an account of a white officer in a black regiment who went before the board, see Levi Lindley Hawes, "Personal Experience of a Union Veteran," *Historic Leaves*, IV (October, 1905), 56–57.

11. Special Orders No. 34, February 24, 1863, in Department of the Gulf, RG 393, pp. 166–67, NA.

12. Captain P. B. S. Pinchback *et al.* to Major General N. P. Banks, March 2, 1863, in Berlin *el al.,* eds., *Freedom,* Ser. II, 321–23.

13. The names of officers who survived their appearance before the board can be determined by comparing the list of officers ordered before the board published in Special Orders No. 34, February 3, 1863, with the dismissals noted in Special Orders No. 55, February 24, 1863, both in Department of the Gulf, RG 393, pp. 120–21 and 166–67, NA.

Lieutenants Octave Rey, Ernest Morphy, and Robert H. Isabelle resigned at the same time for the same reasons.[14]

Most of the other officers in the 2nd Regiment waited to see what would happen. In May, Captain William B. Barrett wrote General Ullmann directly to ask whether he planned to remove all black officers in the process of organizing the Corps d'Afrique. Ullmann responded that he had come "to no determination whatever" in regard to the disposition of black officers. He would wait until he assumed command before making that decision. Barrett decided to stick it out, but eight of his fellow officers saw the handwriting on the wall and decided to resign rather than risk dismissal.[15]

The next wave of resignations from the 2nd Regiment occurred in August, 1863, when the remaining black officers prepared for another round with Banks's examining board, composed of white officers from the same regiment. Incredibly, the white board members were all junior in rank to the black officers whose credentials they would examine. Any dismissals the white board members could effect would allow them to advance in rank, a clear conflict of interest. "A Board of Examination has been formed to investigate the Military Capacity of the *Colored Officers* of this Regiment," Captain Samuel Ringgold protested. "The Officers detailed to compose said Board are in the Majority of inferior rank (Lieutenants of the same Regiment) whose promotion would be effected by our dismissal." Although Brigadier General William H. Emory explained that "when this board was appointed there were no officers of higher rank competent to sit on the board," six black officers in the 2nd Regiment, including Captain Barrett and Major Dumas, resigned rather than submit to this indignity.[16] Only seven black officers were left in the 2nd Regiment.

14. Bertonneau to Captain Wickham Hoffman, March 2, 1863, Morphy to Hoffman, March 3, 1863, and R. H. Isabelle to Hoffman, March 3, 1863, in their Compiled Military Service Records, NA. Octave Rey's resignation can be found in his pension file, also in NA. Both Bertonneau and Rey had served as officers in the Louisiana militia.

15. W. B. Barrett to Ullmann, May 17, 1863, in Barrett's Compiled Military Service Record, NA, also in Berlin *et al.*, eds., *Freedom,* Ser. II, 324; Moses C. Brown (Ullmann's AAG) to Barrett, May 26, 1863, in Barrett's Compiled Military Service Record, NA; *Official Army Register,* VIII, 248; Special Orders No. 126, May 30, 1863, RG 393, pp. 335–36; and Compiled Military Service Records for the eight officers in NA (see Appendix for names).

16. S. W. Ringgold to Banks, July 7, 1863, in Ringgold's Compiled Military Service Record; also Samuel J. Wilkinson to Banks, July 6, 1863, in Wilkinson's Compiled Military Service Record, both in NA. See Compiled Military Service Records and Appendix.

One of the seven who remained was Captain P. B. S. Pinchback, whose company had been detached from the regiment and sent to garrison Fort Pike. Pinchback was the only black officer left at this isolated post, and by mid-September he too had had enough. "I find nearly all the officers inimical to me," he wrote to Banks on September 10, "and I can foresee nothing but dissatisfaction and discontent which will make my position very disagreeable indeed." [17]

Not all of the black officers who left the 2nd Regiment did so for reasons of prejudice. In December, 1863, Second Lieutenant Frank L. Trask left his post as officer of the guard and was found asleep in his bunk. Charges were brought, and Trask was dismissed from the service in February, 1864. Second Lieutenant Solomon Hayes also left the regiment under a cloud. In his letter of resignation dated February 11, 1864, he cited "the prejudice which exists in my Regiment, as well as the entire Service against Colored Officers." The 2nd Regiment's colonel, William M. Grosvenor, was pleased to see him go. "This officer is ignorant, unable to learn, & though a black has neither the respect or confidence of his men," Grosvenor penned in his endorsement. [18]

Hayes's resignation left four black officers in the 2nd Regiment. Captain William Belley was the next to go. On March 31, 1864, he resigned without giving a reason. "After much patient endeavor I have despaired of ever instructing this officer in his duties," Grosvenor noted in his endorsement. "He is one of the original officers of the Regiment," he continued, "and yet, after fourteen months of service as a Captain, is not qualified for examination as second Lieutenant. His ignorance, however, does not so seriously disqualify him, as his mismanagement in the discipline of his company." Grosvenor did not stop there. "In every respect his resignation is, in my judgement[,] a fortunate thing for the Regiment." Regardless of the accuracy of Grosvenor's assessment of Belley's ability, it was getting harder and harder for a black officer in the 2nd Regiment to survive. Captain Joseph Villeverde and First

17. Pinchback to Banks, September 10, 1863, in Pinchback's Compiled Military Service Record, NA.

18. Charges and Specifications preferred against Second Lieutenant Frank L. Trask, of Co. "C" 2d Infantry Corps d'Afrique, December 9, 1863, in Trask's Compiled Military Service Record, NA; Solomon Hayes to Major Drake, February 11, 1864, in Hayes's Compiled Military Service Record, NA, also in Berlin *et al.*, eds., *Freedom*, Ser. II, 326.

Lieutenant Theodule Martin lasted until August, 1864, when they also resigned.[19]

Remarkably, the lone remaining black officer in the 2nd Regiment held on to his commission until the end of the war. He was Charles Sauvenet, the translator in the provost court whom Butler had approached in August, 1862, to discuss reorganizing the Native Guards. Sauvenet must have been an exceptional person, for he was recommended for promotion at a time when Banks was dismissing or forcing the resignations of blacks holding Butler's commissions. Just how Sauvenet survived is unknown. Clearly he was competent, and he served as the regiment's assistant quartermaster, a staff rather than line position. But it is also possible that Sauvenet's light complexion made his continuation in the service more acceptable to his white associates. Butler had described him as "hardly a mulatto."[20] Whatever the case, Sauvenet served three years, making him the black officer with the longest continuous service in the Union army.

The gradual elimination of black officers in the 1st Regiment at Port Hudson followed a similar path, although the first to go did not leave under the best of circumstances. In February, 1863, Captain John De Pass resigned to return to England, his native country, planning to stop in Kingston, Jamaica, on the way to look after property he owned there. Apparently, De Pass was more interested in money than militancy, for Colonel Stafford noted in his endorsement that although De Pass "has sufficient capacity, his carelessness & volatility added to a decided want of principle render him unfit for his present position."[21]

19. Grosvenor's endorsement dated April 5, 1864, in Belley's Compiled Military Service Record, NA. Martin was discharged on August 15, 1864, citing illness (scurvy) as a reason. The reason for Villeverde's resignation is unknown, although he was found deficient in accounting for property for which he was responsible. Information from the officers' Compiled Military Service Records, NA.

20. Sauvenet ended the war as a captain and assistant regimental quartermaster (*Official Army Register,* VIII, 248); Entry dated September 2, 1863, in Sauvenet's Compiled Military Service Record, NA. In May, 1864, Sauvenet's commissary sergeant, P. Flemming, committed suicide, which added to the difficulties of his position (Bearss, *Historic Resource Study,* 221). An inspection report dated March 1, 1865, rated the 74th's arms and equipment as "in good condition," its quarters and barracks as "generally good," and the commissary-quartermaster storehouse as "very good" (*ibid.,* 225). Testimony of Benjamin F. Butler before the American Freedmen's Inquiry Commission, NA.

21. De Pass to Colonel Stafford, February 19, 1863, with Stafford's endorsement of February 22, 1863, in De Pass's Compiled Military Service Record, NA.

By mid-August, 1863, six other black officers in the 1st Regiment had resigned their commissions for the honorable reasons of illness or physical disability.[22] Banks dismissed three in late August.[23] In early September, five black officers who were passed by the examining board were transferred to a new black regiment, the 20th Infantry, Corps d'Afrique.[24] Discouraged by having to leave the regiment in which they had fought and served for the past year and believing this to be a violation of the terms under which they had volunteered, four of the five resigned.[25] The fifth, Captain Charles Sentmanat, held out for a month before resigning as well, citing poor health and the fact that he was the "only remaining colored officer" in the new unit.[26] During September and October, 1863, four more black officers in the 1st Regiment resigned for reasons of ill health or family hardship.[27]

Eight black officers in the 1st Regiment remained. They had been passed by the examining board so it was difficult for Union commanders to complain about their incompetence. Thus when Lieutenants James H. Ingraham and Alfred Bourgeau came up for promotion in October, 1863, Banks did not try to block their advancement. "They have proved themselves thorough and efficient officers," their commander wrote in his recommendation, "and I consider them much better qualified than any we can get, to say nothing of their experience."[28] Nevertheless, the prejudicial treatment of black offi-

22. *Official Army Register*, VIII, 246; and Compiled Military Service Records, NA.

23. Compiled Military Service Records for Hyppolite St. Louis, Louis A. Thibaut, and Alcide Lewis, NA. Lewis was dismissed for cowardice, although the record does not specify an incident. Lewis was the officer about whom Lieutenant John Crowder had complained in a letter to his mother in April.

24. *Official Army Register*, VIII, 246. Banks's organizational plan for the Corps d'Afrique called for regiments of five hundred men instead of the usual thousand (General Orders No. 40, May 1, 1863, *OR*, Vol. XV, pp. 716–17). Because the three regiments comprising the Native Guards had been recruited to full strength, officers and men in excess of fifty per company were transferred to the 20th Regiment, Corps d'Afrique (Bearss, *Historic Resource Study*, 216).

25. Compiled Military Service Records for Edgard Davis, Jules Mallett, Victor Lavinge, and Joseph L. Montieu, NA. Mallett's letter also appears in Berlin, *et al.*, eds., *Freedom*, Ser. II, 327.

26. Eliot Bridgman to G. Norman Lieber, October 4, 1863, in Sentmanat's Compiled Military Service Record, NA.

27. Compiled Military Service Records for Edward Carter, Emile Detiége, Morris W. Morris, and Eugene Rapp, NA. Emile Detiége had been charged with murder on December 12, 1862, for shooting one of his men to death.

28. Lieutenant Colonel C. J. Bassett to Captain G. B. Halstead, October 8, 1863, in Applications for Commissions, Ser. 1936, Pt. 1 [C-1053], NA.

cers continued. "I respectfully tender my immediate and unconditional resignation," Captain Joseph Follin wrote in February, 1864. "Daily events
demonstrate that prejudices are so strong against Colored Officers, that no
matter what would be their patriotism and their anxiety to fight for the flag
of their native Land, they cannot do it with honor to themselves."[29] One by
one, the remaining black officers in the 1st Regiment, the first to volunteer,
resigned, until only Captains James H. Ingraham and Louis A. Snaer remained.[30] Despite being promoted to captain in October, 1863, Ingraham
finally called it quits without giving a reason on March 22, 1864. Like Sauvenet in the 2nd Regiment, Snaer retained his commission to the end of the
war.[31]

Banks's policy of forcing black officers out of the army was shortsighted
in several ways. He failed to use talent that was at his disposal. Banks's own
Inspector General's Office reported in September, 1863, that the 1st Regiment was "partially officered by colored men, some of whom exhibited as
much promptness and intelligence and knowledge of their duties, as a majority of the white officers of other regiments." Colonel John A. Nelson,
commander of the 3rd Regiment, agreed with the inspector general's assessment. Responding to Captain Joseph Oliver's resignation earlier that year,
Nelson described the black man as an "excellent officer" whom I "can
scarcely replace."[32]

Not all of the black officers in the Native Guards acquitted themselves
with honor.[33] Captain Emile Detiége's murder of an enlisted man near Terre-

29. Follin to George B. Drake, February 18, 1864, in Follin's Compiled Service Record,
NA, also in Berlin et al., eds., Freedom, Ser. II, 326.

30. Lieutenant Alfred Bourgeau resigned on March 7, 1863; Captain James Lewis and
Ehurd Moss both resigned a week later (Compiled Military Service Records, NA). Moss resigned to avoid dismissal.

31. Official Army Register, VIII, 246; James H. Ingraham to Richard B. Irwin, March 10,
1864, in Ingraham's Compiled Military Service Record, NA.

32. Inspection Report of 7 cos., 1st Regt. Corps d'Afrique, September 27, 1863, in Regimental Papers, U.S. Colored Troops, Box 44: 69th–75th U.S.C. Inf., RG 94, AGO, NA; Captain
Joseph C. Oliver's Compiled Military Service Record, NA.

33. Andrews' endorsement of Ehurd Moss's resignation read as follows: "This is a colored
officer who is notoriously both incompetent and inefficient. His resignation is probably tendered
to escape being discharged on the recommendation of the Board of Examiners" (Endorsement
of First Lieutenant Ehurd Moss to Lieutenant Colonel Richard B. Irwin, March 8, 1864, in
Berlin et al., eds., Freedom, Ser. II, 328).

bonne Bayou in December, 1862, Captain Alcide Lewis' failure to discipline the exhibitionist at Baton Rouge, and Lieutenant Frank Trask's dismissal for leaving his post as officer of the guard on Ship Island gave evidence that some black officers were unsuited to hold commissions in the Union army. Nevertheless, many of the white officers who replaced them were no better.[34]

Competent white officers who could expect promotion and advancement in their own regiments generally refused assignment to black units.[35] Racism also played its part. "Any [white] man holding a commission in a negro regiment must feel degraded," a Massachusetts soldier wrote home to his brother. Even the bravery of the black troops under fire at Port Hudson did not change these attitudes. "Who would not be a Niggadier General?" the *National Intelligencer* mocked in its report of the Native Guards' assault of May 27.[36] Consequently, many of those who did volunteer were incompetents dissatisfied with their current situation. Furthermore, it was widely known that white commanders unloaded their troublemakers on black companies.[37] Ullmann was disgusted by the hypocrisy of it all. "I well know that those prophets who declare that negroes never will make soldiers," he wrote to Senator Henry Wilson of Massachusetts in December, 1863, "are striving to force their prophecies to work out their own fulfillment by appointing ignoramuses and boors to be officers over men who are as keen-sighted as any to notice the shortcomings of those placed over them. Men have been made field officers in this section who are not fit to be non-commissioned officers—men so ignorant that they cannot write three consecutive sentences without violating orthography and syntax."[38]

There were many examples of poor leadership among the white officers assigned to command the Native Guards.[39] The 1st Regiment's Colonel Staf-

34. Irwin, *Nineteenth Army Corps,* 49–50.

35. For example, see Peter M. Yawyer to his brother, January 10, 1863, in Peter M. Yawyer Letters, LALMVC; also Palfrey, "Port Hudson," 36. There were some exceptions, such as Captain Hiram E. Perkins from the 8th Vermont, who resigned to become a major in the 1st Regiment of the Native Guards (Entry for April 11, 1863, in Kinsley Diary, VHS; and *Official Army Register,* I, 110, VIII, 246).

36. Townsend to his brother, December 15, 1863, MS 280, HNOC; "Negro Troops," *National Intelligencer,* August 24, 1863.

37. Glatthaar, *Forged in Battle,* 31–32, 39–41.

38. Ullmann to Wilson, December 4, 1863, *OR,* Ser. III, Vol. III, p. 1127.

39. In January, 1865, Ullmann was relieved of command at Morganza because a fondness for the bottle made it difficult for him "to give highest attention to the duties devolving upon

ford had been dismissed by court-martial in May, 1863, for "conduct to the prejudice of good order and military discipline."[40] Colonel Nathan W. Daniels of the 2nd Regiment was next. In August, 1863, Daniels and his adjutant, First Lieutenant Elijah K. Prouty, encountered Lieutenant Commander G. A. Perkins of the United States Navy and his wife riding in a carriage in New Orleans. "You say you are riding with a lady," Prouty smirked, "but you are riding with a damned whore." Apparently, Colonel Daniels did not order his adjutant to curb his tongue. "You are a damned shit ass," Prouty continued, "and I room at 122 St. Charles Hotel and will repeat the same thing tomorrow morning." Both Prouty and Daniels surrendered their commissions over this vulgar incident.[41]

Daniels' replacement, Colonel William M. Grosvenor, who hastened the departure of several black officers with harsh evaluations of their competency, lasted until May, 1864, when a general court-martial charged him with "Conduct Unbecoming an Officer and a Gentleman." Grosvenor pleaded guilty to keeping "a woman, not his wife, by the name of 'Belle Fisher'" in his quarters on Ship Island.[42] But he pleaded not guilty to the charge of abusing Assistant Surgeon John H. Gihon of the 2nd Regiment after Gihon intervened when Grosvenor disciplined two black soldiers.[43]

---

him." The officer who brought the order relieving Ullmann of his command reported that he "is full of whiskey all of the time—so much so tonight that he cannot walk steady" (OR, Vol. XLVII, Pt. 1, pp. 677, 984, 986).

40. Stafford's Compiled Military Service Record, NA.

41. The location of this incident must be implied from the letterhead of the stationery used to present the charges and specifications against Lieutenant Prouty, August 19, 1863, in Prouty's Compiled Military Service Record, NA. Daniels was charged with "conduct unbecoming an Officer and a gentleman" by "grossly insulting an Officer of the Navy, while in the company of a lady." Their commissions were revoked in Special Orders No. 384, August 27, 1863, AGO, War Department, in both Daniels' and Prouty's Compiled Military Service Records, NA.

42. General Orders No. 62, Department of the Gulf, May 28, 1864, in *War Record of Col.? W. M. Grosvenor, Editor of the Missouri Democrat* (N.p., n.d., copy in New York Public Library), 2–4. Grosvenor was also charged with keeping "a woman, not his wife, known by the name of 'Jennie Davis,'" in his quarters. Grosvenor pleaded guilty to this charge but attempted to make amends by marrying the woman (*ibid.*, 3).

43. *War Record of Col.? W. M. Grosvenor* spells the Surgeon's name "Gilson," but both Bearss (*Historic Resource Study*), who consulted the original transcript of the trial, and the *Official Army Register* (VIII, 246) use the spelling "Gihon." The incident involved two black soldiers who were locked in the guardhouse for being drunk and disorderly. When they con-

"Now mind, if you or any other Medical Officer ever again dare to interfere with any punishment that I may order to be inflicted," Grosvenor was charged with saying, "I will punish you or him in the same manner, and that within five minutes after, God damn you, Sir, I will let you know that I command this Post." The court found Grosvenor guilty of this charge as well and sentenced him to be dismissed from the service.[44]

Lieutenant Colonel Henry Finnegass of the 3rd Regiment, the coward of Port Hudson, was also dismissed from the service, although his court-martial for "disobedience of orders on the field of battle" hit a snag. Because Colonel Nelson had resigned in August, 1863, to go north, there were no witnesses to Finnegass' insubordination. On September 5, the judge advocate returned the court-martial papers to Brigadier General George L. Andrews, the commander at Port Hudson, stating that he could not bring the accused to trial. The judge advocate's opinion did not deter Andrews from getting rid of Finnegass, even if he could not be court-martialed. Andrews forwarded the paperwork with a strongly worded endorsement. "In my opinion Lieut. Col. Finnegass is in no wise qualified for the position he now holds," Andrews wrote. "His conduct as set forth by his commanding officer, Col. Nelson[,] and the present state of the regiment show clearly that his longer connection with the service will be detrimental thereto. I therefore respectfully recom-

---

tinued to create a disturbance, Grosvenor had them tied and gagged. About midnight, one of the two became very ill. The officer of the guard notified Colonel Grosvenor and sent for Surgeon Gihon. Without consulting Grosvenor, Gihon ordered that the bayonet used as a gag be removed and the soldier taken to the barracks. The surgeon also ordered the other man's gag removed. When the second soldier responded with further ranting and raving, the officer of the guard had the gag replaced and informed Grosvenor of what had happened (Bearss, *Historic Resource Study,* 220).

44. Grosvenor was also charged with abusing the 2nd Regiment's adjutant, Lieutenant F. Burchmore, by threatening him with the following language: "By Jesus Christ, I will put you under arrest; God damn you, Sir, I will let you know that I command this post" (*War Record of Col.? W. M. Grosvenor,* 3). On August 3, 1864, President Lincoln abrogated the sentence "on the ground that the sentence appears not to be sustained by the evidence," but Grosvenor did not rejoin the regiment (Bearss, *Historic Resource Study,* 221–22). Grosvenor went on to an illustrious career following the Civil War. He served as economic editor of the New York *Tribune* from 1875 to 1900, wrote several books on business and finance, and developed an international reputation as America's foremost economist and statistician. He was also gifted in music, literature, mathematics, chess, tennis, and billiards (Walter Williams, "William Mason Grosvenor," in *Dictionary of American Biography* [New York, 1935] VIII, 26–27).

mend that Lieut. Col. Finnegass be discharged from the service of the United States." The War Department in Washington concurred and ordered that Finnegass be dishonorably dismissed from the service.[45]

Weak white officers and the purge of black officers played havoc with the morale among the black enlisted men.[46] After Captain Emile Detiége resigned on September 25, 1863, a fourth of his company deserted. After the last black officer (except Snaer) left the 1st Regiment the following spring, some fifty men deserted. Observing the process of stripping black officers of their commissions from his home in Lowell, Massachusetts, Butler reacted in anger: "The negro, whether the equal to the white man or not, knows when he is treated fairly, and appreciates an injustice quite as endearingly as if of a lighter color." Rhetorically Butler asked, "How can we expect the Black man to stand up against the White rebel when we allow him to be insulted by our own soldier because he [the Union soldier] is White?"[47]

The unfairness of the Union army's treatment of black soldiers was not lost on the men who had been forced to resign. At a mass meeting on November 5, 1863, in New Orleans, P. B. S. Pinchback, formerly a captain in the 2nd Regiment, declared that because black soldiers had fought and died for the Union, they should be allowed to vote. "They did not ask for social equality, and did not expect it," he told the large audience assembled at Economy Hall, "but they demanded political rights—they wanted to become men." Pinchback believed that if blacks were citizens, they should have the right to vote; if not, they should be exempted from the draft.[48]

45. Captain Charles B. Young to Andrews, September 5, 1863, Endorsement to Captain Young's letter of September 5, 1863, dated the same day, and Special Orders No. 122 (extract), March 19, 1864, AGO, War Department, all in Finnegass' Compiled Military Service Record, NA.

46. For problems leading some men to desert, see Warren D. Hamilton to Hon. E. M. Stanton, May, 1865, in Berlin et al., eds., Freedom, Ser. II, 384–85.

47. Official Army Register, VIII, 246; Regimental Books, Civil War, Descriptive Roll of Co. C, 1st Regiment, Native Guards (73rd USCT), RG 94, AGO, NA; Monthly Returns for March and April, 1864, 73rd Inf., USCT, RG 94, NA; Butler to Chase, February 28, 1863, in Butler, Private and Official Correspondence, III, 24; see also Butler's comments regarding Banks's actions in his testimony before the American Freedmen's Inquiry Commission, November 28, 186[3], in Woodward, comp., The Negro in the Military Service of the United States, 2557–62 (M-858, roll 3), NA.

48. "Mass Meeting at Economy Hall," New Orleans Times, November 6, 1863.

Pinchback had a point. Conscription was in effect in Louisiana, and every man of military age was liable to be drafted into the Union army, regardless of his race. Among the exceptions were persons who had already served for two years.[49] The forced resignations of black officers meant that their term of service was less than two years, making them liable to be drafted into the army as privates. Late in the war, seventeen former officers in the Native Guards sought assurances from Banks that they would not be called up for additional service in the army. Banks forwarded their petition to Washington without comment. As expected, the superintendent of the draft refused the petition, citing the requirement for a full two years of service.[50] Fortunately for the black men who had come forward to serve their country in its greatest hour of need only to be discarded, the war was drawing to a close, and the subsequent demobilization of the Union army spared them the ultimate indignity of returning to the ranks of the men they had once commanded.

49. New Orleans *Tribune,* October 25, December 7, 1864; "Revised Regulation for the Government of the Bureau of the Provost-Marshal-General of the United States," *OR,* Ser. III, Vol. IV, p. 658; Enrollment Order No. 1, Department of the Gulf, February 26, 1865, published in the New Orleans *Tribune,* March 12, 1865.

50. "Gallant Officers to Be Put into the Ranks," New Orleans *Tribune,* May 14, 1865.

8

WE SHALL
EVENTUALLY
COME OUT AHEAD

Brigadier General George L. Andrews assumed command of the black troops at Port Hudson on July 10, 1863.[1] Andrews, who did not share many of the prejudices of his fellow officers in the Union army, set to work to make the Corps d'Afrique "one of the best corps in the army."[2] An 1851 graduate of West Point, Andrews finished at the head of his class. After a six-year career as a civil engineer, Andrews returned to the army in 1861 as the lieutenant colonel of the 2nd Massachusetts Infantry. He fought at Cedar Mountain and Antietam in the eastern theater before coming south as Banks's chief of staff in December, 1862.[3]

1. Printed copy of General Orders No. 1 and Andrews to his wife, July 8, 12, 1863, in George L. Andrews Papers, LALMVC; *OR,* Vol. XV, pp. 716–17; Vol. XXVI, Pt. 1, pp. 726, 733; Vol. LIII, p. 561. His was not an enviable assignment. William Dwight thought that Andrews was sacrificing his career by accepting the assignment to command black troops. "[Andrews] is only useful as a tool," Dwight wrote a friend (Dwight to Dan, June 20, 1863, in Dwight Family Papers, MAHS).
2. Samuel M. Quincy to his mother (Mary Jane [Miller] Quincy), November 30, 1863, Quincy to his grandfather (Josiah Quincy), December 5, 1863, both in Quincy, Wendell, Holmes, and Upham Family Papers, LC (microfilm).
3. Warner, *Generals in Blue,* 9.

One of Andrews' first acts as post commander at Port Hudson was to issue General Orders No. 12: "The colored soldier . . . is entitled to respect and consideration, and to the protection and support of his military superiors, particularly when performing any duty which has been imposed on him." Andrews made it clear that "abuse of the colored soldier or opposition to him in the discharge of his duty in this command will be punished with unrelenting severity." Nor did Andrews stop there. "All discussions of the subject of employing colored soldiers, all remarks disparaging them, and any course of conduct tending to create ill-feeling between the colored troops and other troops of this command are most strictly prohibited."[4] Andrews meant business.

Andrews expected officers in the Corps d'Afrique to live up to his high standards. "General Andrews is making excellent troops of the negroes by insisting on the strictest discipline among the officers & showing no mercy to the worthless or incompetent until he gets rid of them," Lieutenant Colonel Samuel M. Quincy of the 1st Regiment wrote to his grandfather.[5] Unlike the situation on Ship Island, Andrews' examining board applied high standards to white officers as well as black. To ensure that those who passed the board continued to upgrade their skills, Andrews established a school for white officers in the Corps d'Afrique and personally supervised their instruction.[6] "He is getting now very good material for officers and is giving them all the instruction & discipline which we received in the 'Second' [Massachusetts]," Quincy noted. "Promotion here will go by merit exclusively. Any officer is now at liberty to apply for promotion upon which he is subjected to a thorough examination before a Board & gets it only if in every respect competent. Many applicants are daily rejected and sent home."[7]

4. Port Hudson, Special Orders No. 12, July 30, 1863, in Woodward, comp., *The Negro in the Military Service of the United States*, 1451–52 (M-858, roll 2), NA.

5. Samuel M. Quincy to his grandfather, December 8, 1863, in Quincy *et al.* Papers, LC. Quincy was a thirty-year-old Harvard-educated lawyer from Boston who had begun his military service as a lieutenant in the 2nd Massachusetts Infantry (Roger D. Hunt and Jack R. Brown, *Brevet Brigadier Generals in Blue* [Gaithersburg, Md., 1990], 496). Quincy's grandfather Josiah P. Quincy had served as a congressman from Massachusetts, mayor of Boston, and president of Harvard University (Joy J. Jackson, "Samuel Miller Quincy," in Glenn R. Conrad, ed., *A Dictionary of Louisiana Biography* [New Orleans, 1988], II, 669).

6. Irwin, *Nineteenth Army Corps*, 261.

7. Samuel M. Quincy to his grandfather, December 5, 1863, in Quincy *et al.* Papers, LC.

Andrews' interest in improving the officer corps was limited to whites only, for the general from Massachusetts did not approve of awarding commissions to blacks. "Few of the colored men I have seen were efficient," he wrote, "and it is not easy to find even those well qualified for non-commissioned officers from lack of education." Although he acknowledged that individual blacks may have been qualified, Andrews objected to black officers in general. "With existing prejudices few or no good white officers will enter a regiment with colored officers," he argued, "and there are not enough colored men who are qualified to fill *all* such positions." Those who were qualified, Andrews believed, "are greatly needed in the non-commissioned staff of the regiments."[8]

Andrews believed that education was the key to turning former slaves into disciplined soldiers. Quincy agreed. "The negroes appear to me," Quincy wrote to his grandfather, "just the material for excellent soldiers under officers whom they respect and fear. Of course," he added, "they have not the self confidence & self respect which makes the educated white man fight[,] even under poor officers like some of our first volunteers."[9] To remedy the situation, Andrews set up schools for almost every regiment, and before long some of the black first sergeants were making out their morning reports without assistance.[10] "You would be much interested in the teaching of our soldiers," Quincy reported. "It seems very queer to see grown men . . . learning their a b abs [*sic*] & making great staggering letters on their slates with great muscular exertion."[11]

So eager were the troops to learn that occasionally it interfered with the

8. Endorsement on request for a commission from Solomon Moses to AAG Geo. B. Drake, Department of the Gulf, November 19, 1864, in Berlin *et al.,* eds., *Freedom,* Ser. II, 331. See also Andrews to Colonel C. C. Dwight (president of the examining board for officers in the Department of the Gulf), November 4, 1863, *ibid.,* 328. By the time Andrews assumed command of Port Hudson, all of the black officers in the 3rd Regiment had resigned. Consequently, Andrews' opinion was formed on the basis of his contact with twenty black officers still serving in the 1st Regiment, several of whom were dismissed from the service by an examining board within weeks of his assuming command.

9. Samuel M. Quincy to his grandfather, December 8, 1863, in Quincy *et al.* Papers, LC.

10. New York *Times,* January 11, 1864; Messner, "Federal Army and Blacks," 384–86. For an extended discussion of the education of black soldiers, see John W. Blassingame, "The Union Army as an Educational Institution for Negroes, 1862–1865," *Journal of Negro Education,* XXXIV (1965), 152–59.

11. Quincy to his mother, March 12, 1864, in Quincy *et al.* Papers, LC.

performance of other duties. "This afternoon I observed a relief marching off guard at the parapet & the last man lagging behind," Quincy wrote to his mother. "I rode up intending to blow him sky high, but when I got there found that he had his gun in his right hand & his spelling book in his left & was so intent on the latter that he didn't see where he was going." Quincy stopped a moment to consider and let the incident pass.[12]

Despite efforts to improve themselves, the men in Corps d'Afrique were still treated as second-class soldiers in the Union army. This was evident on a Saturday afternoon in early October, 1863, when they fell into formation to draw their pay. Much to their chagrin, the rate of pay was only $10 per month, of which $3 was deducted for uniforms.[13] White soldiers were paid $13 and got to keep it all. The officers, most of whom were white by now, received the same pay as officers in white units.[14] Because many of the men had families to support and because they had gone for almost six months without being paid anything, they grudgingly took the money. Major John C. Chadwick, a white officer in one of the black regiments stationed at Port Hudson, protested the unfair treatment.

They have been mustered into the service of the United States as soldiers; they have been called upon, and still are, to do all the duties of such, and to undergo all the hardships and privations, as such. And they were told that they were to receive the same pay as white troops; told by their officers that they were to receive the pay of their grades in accordance with the regulations for the government of the armies of the United States. It does not seem to be in accordance with the

12. Quincy to his grandfather, December 8, 1863, *ibid.* Quincy had good reason to be concerned. Maintaining discipline among the black troops at Port Hudson was difficult, as it is with any troops on garrison duty (see Samuel Roosa to Abraham Lincoln, January 24, 1864, in Berlin *et al.,* eds., *Freedom,* Ser. II, 477–79).

13. "An Act to amend the act calling forth the militia etc.," July 17, 1862, *OR,* Ser. III, Vol. II, pp. 281–82; also Ullmann to H. Wilson, December 4, 1863, *OR,* Ser. III, Vol. III, pp. 1126–27. The militia act gave the president authority "to receive into the service of the United States, for the purpose of constructing entrenchments, or performing camp service, or any other labor, or any military or naval service for which they may be found competent, persons of African descent." Initially viewed as laborers for the army, blacks were paid less than soldiers. Eventually, the provisions of the act were expanded to permit their use as soldiers, although their pay remained at its initial level.

14. Field and Staff Muster Roll, September and October, 1863, 74th U.S. Col'd Inf., Compiled Military Service Records, NA.

principles of justice, equity, and honor, that these soldiers of the United States Army, should receive less pay per month, for the same services, than any other United States Soldiers of the same grade and class; and in their name and on their behalf, I most earnestly and respectfully protest, and pray that this evident injustice may be speedily rectified, that the seeds of discord and discontent may not be sown or take root.[15]

It took eight months, until mid-June, 1864, before the pay situation was resolved. Under pressure from northern politicians, some Union commanders, and white officers serving in black regiments, Congress finally authorized equal pay for all soldiers, black and white.[16] But even then, Congress' remedy was prejudicial. Black soldiers who had been free on April 19, 1861, were eligible for back pay equal to that for white soldiers of the same rank. The black man who had been a slave on that date was not accorded the same right. This caused another howl of protest, but it was March, 1865, before Congress passed a law that granted equal pay for all black soldiers starting at the time of their enlistment.[17] Even then, some members of the Corps d'Afrique did not receive the bounty they had been promised when they enlisted in the Native Guards until 1867.[18]

The black soldiers at Port Hudson grumbled about their pay but returned to the daily grind of garrison duty. The boredom was broken temporarily by a big party on Christmas Day, 1863. "We, i.e., the American soldiers of African descent, climbed greased poles, chased greased pigs[,] road [sic] mules wherein everybody rode another man's mule & the last one in beat,"

15. John C. Chadwick to Banks, October 3, 1863, in Woodward, comp., *The Negro in the Military Service of the United States,* 1657 (M-858, roll 2), NA (quotation); Westwood, "Benjamin Butler's Enlistment of Black Troops," 22.

16. For an example of political pressure for equal pay, see John A. Andrew (governor of Massachusetts) to Lincoln, March 24, 1864, *OR,* Ser. III, Vol. IV, pp. 274–77.

17. General Orders No. 215, June 22, 1864, *OR,* Ser. III, Vol. IV, p. 448; General Orders No. 31, March 8, 1865, *ibid.,* 1223; also see Edwin Bates to Lincoln, July 24, 1864, *ibid.,* 490–93, and the Final Report of the Provost-Marshal-General's Bureau, March 17, 1866, *OR,* Ser. III, Vol. V, pp. 657–59; also Glatthaar, *Forged in Battle,* 174–75. Some officers allowed black soldiers who had been slaves on or before April 19, 1861, to circumvent the reduced pay policy by asserting their free status under the terms of a "Quaker Oath" (*i.e.,* a false declaration permitted on the assumption that the soldiers were appealing to God's law, which was based on a higher authority than that promulgated by the secretary of war) (William A. Gladstone, *Men of Color* [Gettysburg, Pa., 1993], 98–99).

18. New Orleans *Republican,* May 11, 1867.

Lieutenant Colonel Quincy wrote to his mother. The black troops also "had wheelbarrow races blindfolded & indulged in all sorts of intellectual pastimes combining amusement & instruction." But the party was soon over, and "we are now hard at work again," Quincy wrote, "& for the last week I have been inspecting two regiments a day, which is about work enough for one man." [19]

Entertainment that the black troops could fashion for themselves was about all they could get.[20] A musical band that had been assembled in Boston especially for the Corps d'Afrique was waylaid in New Orleans. "The pleasure loving officers at Headquarters and on detached service are having a splendid series of promenade concerts at our expense," a correspondent at Port Hudson protested to his readers in the New York *Tribune*. "Is not enough," he complained, "that they have a Theater, Opera House, Galpin's, the Globe ball-room, Dan Hickak's, and other places of enjoyment, without robbing us who are in the field of our only luxury?"[21] Quincy remarked on the incident as well. "They took away our band & are keeping them at New Orleans. What do the old niggers & their officers want such a good band for[?]" he wrote sarcastically to his mother. Quincy went on to complain of

19. Quincy to his mother, December 29, 1863, in Quincy *et al.* Papers, LC.

20. Black soldiers in the Department of the Gulf were not allowed "to leave their camp, or to wander through the parishes, except upon written permission, or in the company of their officers" (General Orders, August 21, 1863, in the New Orleans *Daily Picayune,* August 28, 1863; also see *Liberator,* February 26, 1864). White soldiers, by contrast, were given permission to hunt or fish at will (Special Orders No. 45 [not in *OR*], quoted in *The Letter H, the Camp Newspaper for Co. H, 26th Conn. Inf.,* Vol. I, No. 1, March 2, 1863, Camp Parapet, La., in Bennett Letters, HNOC).

21. New York *Tribune,* February 10, 1864. The St. Charles Theater was on St. Charles Avenue at Poydras near Lafayette Park in the American sector of the city, while the French Opera House, built in 1859, stood on the corner of Bourbon and Toulouse in the French sector (John B. Garvey and Mary Lou Widmer, *Beautiful Crescent: A History of New Orleans* [New Orleans, 1982], 85). John Galpin's restaurant was located at 9 Exchange Place just off Canal Street (Gardner, *Gardner's New Orleans Directory for 1861,* 184). Today there are two eating establishments on Exchange Place—a Burger King and a New Orleans Famous Fried Chicken restaurant. Dan Hickok's Hotel (correct spelling) was a fashionable watering spot at the lake end of the New Basin Canal on the present site of the Southern Yacht Club (Garvey and Widmer, *Beautiful Crescent,* 90). The Globe Ball Room was located on the corner of St. Peter and Basin streets across from the Old Basin, where the Municipal Auditorium stands today (New Orleans *Tribune,* December 13, 1865). The Globe was one of the many "Brothel Ball Rooms" catering to the baser instincts of the Federal troops.

the treatment of black troops in general. "It is an undoubted fact that the authorities here are opposed to our success and will not treat either officers or men as on equality with other troops." But at this point during the war Quincy was still optimistic. "But with Uncle Sam to back us," he asserted, "I am not afraid to toy conclusions with anybody & believe that we shall eventually come out ahead."[22]

Time for bands and parties was soon forgotten as the men of the Corps d'Afrique began to prepare for the active campaigning that was sure to come with the warm spring weather. In early March, 1864, Colonel William H. Dickey assumed command of the brigade to which the 1st and 3rd Regiments were assigned. Although its "arms are poor," Andrews reported to Banks's headquarters that Dickey's brigade was ready for the field. Two weeks later, the black troops traveled by water from Port Hudson to the mouth of the Red River and eventually to Alexandria, arriving on March 23. The day after their arrival, Banks's assistant adjutant general made sure that Dickey's men understood their place. "You will keep your brigade well in hand," he ordered, "and grant no passes until you are established in camp. Non-commissioned officers and privates [*i.e.*, blacks in uniform] are noticed on the streets, which must be stopped at once."[23]

On March 29, Banks started his army toward Grand Ecore, a small village on the bluffs overlooking the Red River. Nine days later, Banks continued his movement toward Shreveport. Dickey's brigade brought up the rear, protecting a portion of the army's long wagon train. The next day, the black troops reached Pleasant Hill while the head of Banks's column pushed on toward a vital crossroads near Mansfield, Louisiana.[24]

On April 9, General Richard Taylor's Confederate army tore into the vanguard of Banks's men at Mansfield. The Union troops fell back but found their way blocked by wagons abandoned by teamsters who had fled to the rear. As the Confederates pressed their aggressive attack, the retreating col-

22. Quincy to his mother, July 8, 1864, in Quincy *et al.* Papers, LC.

23. Andrews to C. P. Stone, March 1, 1864, *OR*, Vol. XXXIV, Pt. 2, p. 474; also Vol. XXXIV, Pt. 1, p. 171; C. P. Stone to Banks, March 23, 1864, *OR*, Vol. XXXIV, Pt. 1, p. 179; George B. Drake to Dickey, March 24, 1864, *OR*, Vol. XXXIV, Pt. 2, p. 716.

24. Ludwell H. Johnson, *Red River Campaign: Politics and Cotton in the Civil War* (1958; rpr. Gaithersburg, Md., 1986), 124–25; also *OR*, Vol. XXXIV, Pt. 1, p. 199, 201; Vol. XXXIV, Pt. 2, p. 676; Vol. XXXIV, Pt. 3, pp. 35, 58, 452.

umns turned into a "disorganized mob of screaming, sobbing, hysterical, pale, terror-stricken men."[25] The rout continued for several miles until the demoralized soldiers reached a ridge where Brigadier General William H. Emory established a strong defensive position. Emory's line held through the night, but Banks had decided to continue his retreat to Pleasant Hill. As the Union troops dug in, Banks ordered the long wagon train, or what was left of it, to continue on the road toward Grand Ecore guarded by some demoralized cavalry and Dickey's brigade of black soldiers.[26]

The wagon train reached Grand Ecore on April 10, and Dickey's brigade immediately began fortifying the position. Meanwhile, Banks and Taylor were slugging it out at Pleasant Hill, approximately thirty miles to the west. Although the battle at Pleasant Hill was tactically a Union victory, Banks retreated to Grand Ecore, where he halted briefly before falling back to Alexandria. Banks wanted to get out of central Louisiana altogether but had to stay in Alexandria if he was to save the navy.[27] Low water in the Red River meant that the rapids, which had been difficult to cross on the trip upriver, were impossible to traverse on the return. A dozen navy vessels were trapped above the rapids as a result of record low water levels in the channel.[28]

One of Banks's engineers, Lieutenant Colonel Joseph Bailey, believed that he could construct wing dams from the shore that would back up the water in the main channel sufficiently to allow the gunboats to pass. Under Bailey's direction, men from New England regiments familiar with lumbering felled trees while other soldiers worked with stone taken from an old quarry. Other troops tore down fences and buildings and seized cotton gin and sugar house machinery to construct the dams. Sailors lightened the ships by removing all of the guns and stores and as much of the armor as possible. Dickey's brigade

25. Flinn, *Campaigning with Banks in Louisiana*, 108–109.

26. *Report of the Joint Committee on the Conduct of the War, at the Second Session Thirty-Eighth Congress*, Vol. II, *Red River Campaign* (Washington, D.C., 1865), 12; Beecher, *Record of the 114th Regiment*, 311–14; also *OR*, Vol. XXXIV, Pt. 1, pp. 354, 423.

27. Banks to Mary Banks, April 20, 1864, in Banks Collection, LC.

28. Johnson, *Red River Campaign*, 220–21; David D. Porter to William T. Sherman, April 16, 1864, *OR*, Vol. XXXIV, Pt. 3, pp. 169–74; also *OR*, Vol. XXXIV, Pt. 1, pp. 189–92; *Official Records of the Union and Confederate Navies in the War of the Rebellion* (30 vols.; Washington, D.C., 1894–1927), Ser. I, Vol. XXVI, pp. 92–95, 130–35.

helped strengthen the defensive perimeter, which allowed the troops under Bailey to devote full attention to the work.[29]

The fleet made it successfully over the rapids by May 12, and Banks continued his retreat.[30] Four days later, the Union column encountered a strong force of Confederate cavalry and artillery at Mansura, blocking the road. The Union army formed a line of battle to force the Rebels out of the way. Dickey's brigade was positioned in the center of the line. It was a bright, sunlit morning, one of those remarkable occasions when the weather and the terrain offered spectators the opportunity to see an entire army without obstruction. Some men from the 13th Connecticut, which had been held in reserve, sat on top of a fence to watch the spectacle. "Almost the whole army was seen, resplendent in steel and brass," one of the men wrote. "Miles of lines and columns; the cavalry gliding over the ground in the distance with a delicate, nimble lightness of innumerable twinkling feet; a few batteries enveloped in smoke and incessantly thundering, others dashing swiftly to salient positions; division and corps commanders with their staff officers clustering about them, watching through their glasses the hostile army; couriers riding swiftly from wing to wing; everywhere the beautiful silken flags; and the scene ever changing with the involutions and evolutions of the vast host!"[31]

Firing, mostly by artillery, continued for four hours until Union reinforcements arrived. The Confederates fell back, opening the road and allowing Banks's army to continue its retreat. Casualties were light on both sides, and the black soldiers in Dickey's brigade returned to their customary role as guards for the Union wagon train. Banks's army reached Simmesport on

29. Johnson, *Red River Campaign*, 260–66; *OR*, Vol. XXXIV, Pt. 1, pp. 209–10, 402–404; *Report of the Joint Committee on the Conduct of the War*, 15–16; Flinn, *Campaigning with Banks in Louisiana*, 135–36. On May 6 Banks ordered Dickey to detach his "largest and best regiment" to help with the construction (*OR*, Vol. XXXIV, Pt. 3, p. 474). But Bailey did not include any of Dickey's regiments in his list of troops who helped construct the dams (*OR*, Vol. XXXIV, Pt. 1, pp. 404–405).

30. *Report of the Joint Committee on the Conduct of the War*, 332–33.

31. R. Taylor to S. S. Anderson, May 16, 1864, *OR*, Vol. XXXIV, Pt. 1, pp. 592–93; Map of Battle of Mansura, *ibid.*, 235; John C. Becht's report, May 25, 1864, *ibid.*, 325; Homer B. Sprague, *History of the 13th Infantry Regiment of Connecticut Volunteers During the Great Rebellion* (Hartford, Conn., 1867), 212.

May 21.[32] The campaign was at an end, and the 1st and 3rd Regiments of the Corps d'Afrique returned to Port Hudson briefly before being reassigned to Morganza, Louisiana, where they would spend the next eight months. Meanwhile, the 2nd Regiment continued its solitary duty guarding military convicts on Ship Island in the Gulf of Mexico.[33]

32. T. A. Faries' report, May 17, 1864, *OR,* Vol. XLIII, Pt. 1, pp. 630–31; Dickey's report, May 27, 1864, *OR,* Vol. XXXIV, Pt. 1, p. 443, also pp. 193, 591–95.

33. Field and Staff Muster Roll, May, 1864, to January, 1865, Compiled Unit Records, 73rd and 75th U.S. Col'd Inf., NA; Field and Staff Muster Roll, May, 1864, to September, 1865, Compiled Unit Records, 74th U.S. Col'd Inf., NA.

9

DIGGERS AND
DRUDGES

During the Red River campaign only three black officers still held commissions in the Corps d'Afrique. This did not mean, however, that those who had resigned were sitting quietly on the sidelines. As the black enlisted men trudged through the countryside of central Louisiana, their former officers were busy in New Orleans organizing a fledgling civil rights movement that hoped to capitalize on the promise of emancipation and the removal of the old political power elite, which was sure to result with the collapse of Confederate resistance.[1]

One of the first meetings of the new movement occurred in January, 1864, when a large group of black men assembled in Economy Hall to press for the right to vote. Believing that Lincoln would be sympathetic to their cause, they decided to send two delegates to Washington to present a petition asking that black men in Louisiana be enfranchised. The delegates they chose were Jean Baptiste Roudanez, an engineer, and Arnold Bertonneau, formerly a captain in the 2nd Regiment of the Corps d'Afrique.[2]

1. The political ramifications of black soldiers in the Union army had been recognized as early as September, 1862, when the 1st Regiment of the Native Guards was sworn into service (Logsdon and Bell, "Americanization of Black New Orleans," 221–22).
2. McCrary, *Abraham Lincoln and Reconstruction,* 229–30; also Logsdon and Bell, "Amer-

Roudanez and Bertonneau met with Lincoln in Washington on March 12, the same day the 1st and 3rd Regiments left Port Hudson to begin their journey up the Red River to Alexandria. Although he remained noncommittal on the question of black suffrage, Lincoln wrote a brief letter to Michael Hahn, a moderate Unionist who had been elected governor of Louisiana only a few weeks before. Noting that a convention to revise the state's constitution was about to convene, Lincoln raised the question of whether blacks would be granted suffrage in the new document. "I barely suggest, for your private consideration," Lincoln wrote Hahn, "whether some of the colored people may not be let in [*i.e.*, enfranchised], as, for instance, the very intelligent, and especially those who have fought gallantly in our ranks. They would probably help, in some trying time to come, to keep the jewel of liberty in the family of freedom." [3]

Unaware of the president's letter to Hahn, Roudanez and Bertonneau continued to press their case with other powerful leaders in the North. While in Washington, they met with the famous antislavery advocate and senator from Massachusetts, Charles Sumner, and then traveled to Boston to confer with abolitionists William Lloyd Garrison, Wendell Phillips, and Frederick Douglass. On April 12 the two delegates from Louisiana attended a dinner in their honor at the Parker House, Boston's finest hotel. The host was John Andrew, governor of Massachusetts, who introduced Bertonneau to the guests and asked him to make some remarks. The former captain in the Corps d'Afrique spoke warmly of Benjamin Butler's administration of New Orleans after the city's surrender. "We felt that we were men and citizens, and were to be treated as such," Bertonneau told his audience. "We were animated by new hopes and new desires; we felt that there was a new life opened before us; so we gave our imagination full scope and play." Bertonneau then went on to chronicle the contributions black men in Louisiana had made to the war effort, particularly those in the Corps d'Afrique. Predicting that the war would not last much longer, Bertonneau drew attention to the future. "The right to vote must be secured," he asserted. "The doors of our public schools must be opened, that our children, side by side, may

---

icanization of Black New Orleans," 226–27. When Bertonneau resigned in March, 1863, the 2nd Regiment was still designated as the Native Guards.

3. *Ibid.,* 255–56; Lincoln to Hahn, March 13, 1864, New Orleans *Daily Picayune,* July 6, 1865. This letter was confidential, and Hahn did not release its contents until after Lincoln's death more than a year later.

study from the same books, and imbibe the same principles and precepts from the Book of Books—learn the great truth that God 'created of one blood all nations of man to dwell on the face of the earth'—so will caste, founded on prejudice against color, disappear."[4] Applause, cheers, and a toast to Ben Butler at the end of his speech gave evidence of the eloquence with which Bertonneau had moved his audience.

Back at Port Hudson, the end of the Red River campaign brought new unit designations to the Corps d'Afrique. Almost a year earlier, the War Department in Washington had established the Bureau of Colored Troops with responsibility for enrolling and training all black soldiers in the Union army. Under the direction of Major Charles W. Foster, the bureau detailed inspectors to the field, supervised examining boards for officer selection, and established a uniform system of training. As the enlistment of black troops gained momentum, the bureau decided to renumber all the black regiments in the Union army. The result was the creation of a new designation, United States Colored Troops (USCT), and the 1st, 2nd, and 3rd Regiments of Banks's Corps d'Afrique became the 73rd, 74th, and 75th Infantry USCT, respectively.[5]

The change in unit designations did not alter the army's decision to use black soldiers primarily as common laborers. The policy was the result of a deeply ingrained prejudice against blacks among many Union generals, including the commander of the Department of the Gulf.[6] In organizing the Corps d'Afrique Banks had expressed confidence that the new corps "will render important service to the Government." What he had in mind, however, was "not established upon any dogma of equality or other theory, but as a practical and sensible matter of business. The Government makes use of mules, horses, uneducated and educated white men, in the defense of

4. "Dinner to Citizens of Louisiana," *Liberator,* April 5, 1864.

5. General Orders 144, May 22, 1863, *OR,* Ser. III, Vol. III, pp. 215–16; Orders No. 16, War Department, April 4, 1864, *OR,* Ser. III, Vol. IV, p. 215; also General Orders No. 51, Department of the Gulf, April 19, 1864, *OR,* Vol. XXXIV, Pt. 3, p. 221.

6. New York *Times,* March 8, 1863; William F. Smith and James T. Brady, "Commission on Corrupt Practices in the South, Final Report, Sept. 23, 1865," 52, 54, in RG 94, AGO, NA; George S. Denison to Salmon P. Chase, February 26, 1863, in Chase, "Diary and Correspondence," 361. Brigadier General Charles P. Stone, Banks's new chief of staff, made a clear distinction between black troops and "good troops" (Stone to Banks, November 13, 1863, *OR,* Vol. XXVI, Pt. 1, p. 798).

its institutions," Banks observed. "Why should not the negro contribute whatever is in his power for the cause in which he is as deeply interested as other men?"[7] As far as Banks was concerned, the black soldiers could contribute through their ability to perform hard duty, such as "throwing up defensive earthworks, a kind of labor always unwillingly performed by white troops."[8] Thus, while white soldiers cleaned their equipment and drilled, black soldiers were kept busy digging ditches and latrines, loading and unloading supplies, strengthening defensive positions, and standing guard.[9]

Another reason black troops were used extensively for fatigue duty was the erroneous assumption that blacks were immune to the pestilence that struck down so many white Northern troops in the semitropical climate of Louisiana. "I rather like the notion [of forming the Corps d'Afrique]," a Union soldier from Connecticut wrote his family in 1863, "for niggers are the only troops that are fitted to live in this country." A captain in the 53rd Massachusetts Infantry thought the same: "They are servisable any where. The[y] can be put into the unhealthy localities in the department and not suffer like white men."[10]

They were wrong. Black soldiers were dropping like flies.[11] During August, 1864, 524 out of 652 enlisted men in the 4th Cavalry USCT stationed at Port Hudson were "taken sick." Of these, 243 suffered from intermittent fever and 147 from diarrhea. Two of the latter group died. These illnesses

---

7. General Orders No. 40, May 1, 1863, Department of the Gulf, in *OR,* Vol. XV, p. 717.

8. New York *Times,* February 23, 1863. Also see Samuel Clark to Daniel Ullmann, August 11, 1863, in Daniel Ullmann Papers, Reel 4, Frame 323, NYHS.

9. Babcock, ed., *Selections from Letters and Diaries,* 104; Randall C. Jimerson, *The Private Civil War: Popular Thought During the Sectional Conflict* (Baton Rouge, 1988), 93; Ripley, *Slaves and Freedmen in Civil War Louisiana,* 118–19; David Hunter Strother, *A Virginia Yankee in the Civil War: The Diaries of David Hunter Strother,* ed. Cecil D. Eby (Chapel Hill, 1961), 154; John L. Rice to AAG, July 20, 1864, in Berlin *et al.,* eds., *Freedom,* Ser. II, 506–507.

10. Charles Bennett to his family, May 8, 1863, in Bennett Letters, HNOC; Anson D. Fessenden to his parents from New Orleans, April 18, 1863, in Anson D. Fessenden Papers, LALMVC. For a similar opinion, see a correspondent's report to the New York *Times* reprinted in Wilson, *Black Phalanx,* 526.

11. The death rate among black soldiers from disease was more than twice as high as that for white soldiers (William F. Fox, *Regimental Losses in the American Civil War, 1861–1865* [Albany, 1889], 49).

were in addition to the threat of death or injury from the accidental discharge of firearms, which killed one man, and being struck by lightning, which killed another. September was just as bad; three soldiers in the 4th Cavalry died from diarrhea, three from dysentery, and two from pneumonia. Only when cooler weather came in October did the incidence of fever and diarrhea fall, although many men continued to die from illnesses contracted during the summer months. August seemed the worst month for sickness, especially for the 74th USCT stationed on Ship Island in the Gulf.[12]

The high rate of sickness among the black troops was exacerbated by the shortage of competent physicians to provide medical care. Banks wrote to Washington in July, 1864, to complain that "there was a serious want of Surgeons." Competent surgeons declined to serve with black troops. "It was impossible to get good [medical] officers to accept such commissions," he wrote. As a result, hospital stewards were appointed to the posts of assistant surgeon and surgeon in the black regiments, where they performed many duties for which they were not qualified, including surgery. Banks tried to correct the situation by recruiting recent graduates from medical schools in the Northeast. Although this strategy met with some success, the lack of adequate medical care in the black regiments persisted to the end of the war.[13]

Despite illness and disease, the tendency to use black troops primarily as common laborers became so widespread that Ullmann wrote to Senator Henry Wilson to complain that "many high officials outside of Washington have no other intention than that these men shall be used as diggers and drudges." Lieutenant Colonel Quincy shared Ullmann's appraisal. "Colored troops . . . are mostly employed in the dirty work of the army & not given a chance to fight," he wrote to his mother in late April, 1864. The disparity continued until mid-June, 1864, when Secretary of War Stanton ordered his field commanders to divide fatigue duty equally between black and white troops.[14]

---

12. Report of Sick and Wounded by Surgeon D[aniel] D. Slauson, 4th U.S. C[ol-ored].C[avalry], from August, 1864, at Port Hudson, Louisiana, in D. D. Slauson Papers, LALMVC; Monthly Returns for the 73rd, 74th, and 75th Inf., USCT, NA. Returns for the 74th are complete. There is a six-month break in the returns for the 73rd (June, August–December, 1863), and the returns for the 75th are available beginning in September, 1863.

13. Banks to Major C. T. Chirstenen, July 18, 1864, in Woodward, comp., *The Negro in the Military Service of the United States*, 2694–95 (M-858, roll 3), NA.

14. Ullmann to Wilson, December 4, 1863, *OR*, Ser. III, Vol. 3, p. 1127; Quincy to his

The reprieve from constant fatigue duty did not bring relief from the drudgery of garrison life. The day began at five-thirty with the beating of drums. Reveille was at six, at which time the black troops would fall in by companies at parade rest in two ranks facing each other. After roll call, those who had become sick during the night reported to the surgeon; the remainder returned to their tents to prepare for the day's duties. Breakfast was at seven o'clock, the camp guard for the day was posted at seven-thirty, and the men assembled for drill at eight. Drill lasted for an hour and a half, after which the troops were dismissed for various details until dinner call at one o'clock. There was another hour and a half of drill in the afternoon starting at three-thirty. Late afternoon was devoted to inspection and a parade. The men generally had the evening free unless they were on guard duty. They assembled in two ranks again for tattoo at nine o'clock. At this formation the first sergeants called out the names of the men assigned to details on the following day. Taps sounded at nine-thirty, at which time all lights were extinguished and silence prevailed.[15]

The drudgery of garrison duty for the 73rd USCT at Port Hudson was broken, if only temporarily, by a dress review to celebrate the Fourth of July. The parade went smoothly, but even this diversion from the boredom of camp life was anticlimactic. There was no one to witness the event. "A review looks funny without any spectators," Quincy wrote his mother, "drums beating[,] colors flying—everybody galloping around in full uniform apparently for the edification of two contrabands & a mule."[16]

On July 24, the 74th USCT on Ship Island was merged with the 91st USCT to bring the 74th up to its authorized strength. Following the merger, five companies remained on Ship Island, three continued to garrison Fort Pike, and the remaining two were posted to Fort McComb. Within a month, however, three of the five companies on Ship Island were detached for service against Fort Morgan at the mouth of Mobile Bay. Freed from the drudgery

mother, April 25, 1864, in Quincy et al. Papers, LC; Orders No. 21, War Department, June 14, 1864, OR, Ser. III, Vol. IV, p. 431; also published in the New Orleans Tribune, September 13, 1864. Banks issued the same orders two months later over his signature, giving the impression that he was responsible for this enlightened policy (General Orders No. 108 [printed], Department of the Gulf, August 5, 1864, in Banks Collection, LC).

15. Samuel M. Quincy, A Camp and Garrison Manual for Volunteers and Militia (New Orleans, 1865), 6–18.

16. Quincy to his mother, July 8, 1864, in Quincy et al. Papers, LC.

of constant fatigue duty, eight of the ten companies of the 74th, including the three sent to Mobile, had been trained in the use of heavy artillery. Now these skills were needed on Mobile Point, where the Union army was attempting to batter Fort Morgan into submission. The three companies landed on the Alabama coast on August 21, just in time to witness the capitulation of the Rebel fortress two days later. By early September, the three companies were back on Ship Island, manning the guns of Fort Massachusetts.[17]

Back at Morganza, the 75th joined two white regiments and another black one, the 92nd USCT, on an expedition to Simmesport in mid-September to prevent a Confederate raiding party from escaping across the Atchafalaya. The expedition failed in its mission, and during the return march troops from the 92nd broke ranks to steal chickens and other items from local inhabitants. The expedition's commander halted the unauthorized plundering and singled out the 75th in his report for exemplary behavior. "The Seventy-fifth Colored Infantry is an excellently behaved regiment," he wrote, "and I could not but admire their good behavior while the Ninety-second were straggling about houses and yards this morning."[18]

In December, 1864, the 73rd joined the 92nd USCT on a similar foray. Using curses, vilification, and blows, the white officers made certain there would be no straggling this time. The discipline was so severe that the 73rd's chaplain, Samuel L. Gardner, complained to Ullmann. Noting that such treatment would not be tolerated by white soldiers, Gardner argued that "the discipline of the service ought to present to them [black troops] a contrast to the irresponsible cruelties of slavedriving, instead of a too faithful reproduction of them."[19]

The next few months passed uneventfully, but by February, 1865, things began to stir. Major General Edward R. S. Canby, who had replaced Banks as commander of the Department of the Gulf, began making plans to capture the last Confederate stronghold on the Gulf Coast—Mobile, Alabama. He picked the 73rd USCT to participate in the campaign, one of only two black regiments from Morganza selected for the honor.[20] On February 26, the 73rd

17. Bearss, *Historic Resource Study,* 223, 212, 224.

18. J. J. Guppey's report, September 18, 1864, *OR,* Vol. XLI, Pt. 1, p. 805.

19. Samuel L. Gardner to General D. Ullman[n], December 19, 1864, in Berlin *et al.,* eds., *Freedom,* Ser. II, 417–18.

20. Special Orders No. 52, February 21, 1865, *OR,* Vol. XLVIII, Pt. 1, pp. 926–27, also pp. 954, 985.

left for Pensacola, where it was brigaded with two other black regiments under the command of Brigadier General William Anderson Pile.[21]

Pile's brigade began its advance toward Mobile on March 20.[22] Two formidable strongholds, Spanish Fort and Fort Blakely, protected the city. Pile's men reached Fort Blakely on April 1. The next morning Pile threw out his skirmishers and inched to within nine hundred yards of the Confederate fortifications. Having advanced as far as possible without making an all-out assault, the black soldiers began the backbreaking work of digging approaches to the Rebel position. For almost a week they did what they were accustomed to doing, throwing dirt. But this time there was a reason: to protect themselves from the constant fire from Rebel sharpshooters. By the morning of April 9, Pile's men were close enough to charge the Rebel fortifications when ordered. At noon the Confederate sniping stopped, and everything suddenly became quiet. The commander of the 73rd, Lieutenant Colonel Henry C. Merriam, sent a message to Pile asking permission to push his skirmishers forward to feel out the enemy. Pile ordered a section of two artillery pieces to throw some shells into the Confederate lines to determine whether they were still occupied. The guns fired several rounds, but there was no reply. Pile decided to let Merriam's men move forward.[23]

The ground between the 73rd's position and Fort Blakely was level but badly cut up by deep ravines. The Confederates had protected their positions well with a strong abatis of slashed timber. Approximately five hundred yards in front of the main line, the Confederates had dug a series of rifle pits. The men sprang forward as the Confederates opened fire with rifles and cannon. Using the broken ground for cover, the black troops reached the rifle pits and captured several Confederate sharpshooters before they could escape back to their own lines. The Rebels in the fort concentrated a heavy fire on the black soldiers, who dug in behind the tree trunks and limbs in front of the Confederate position.[24]

At 5:45 P.M., the Union troops on the left advanced for a final assault. Pile ordered his brigade forward, and the 73rd USCT rushed toward the

21. Organization of the Union forces commanded by Maj. Gen. R. S. Canby, operating against Mobile, Ala., March 17–April 12, *OR*, Vol. XLIX, Pt. 1, p. 108.

22. Itinerary of the Army of West Mississippi, *ibid.*, 135.

23. Pile's report, April 13, 1865, *ibid.*, 288–89.

24. Reports of Lieutenant Colonel D. Densmore, 68th USCT, and Major W. E. Nye, 76th USCT, in Woodward, comp., *The Negro in the Military Service of the United States*, 4105, 4107 (M-858, roll 3), NA; also Pile's report, *OR*, Vol. XLIX, Pt. 1, p. 289.

Confederate fortifications. The abatis slowed them down, but the black soldiers kept going. Fortunately, most of the Confederate rife fire passed overhead.[25] Within minutes the black troops captured seven pieces of artillery and some prisoners. Some of the Confederates ran toward a white Union division on the left to avoid being captured by black soldiers. They need not have worried, for Pile's men exhibited "excellent discipline" and treated their captives as prisoners of war.[26] "To the Seventy-third U.S. Colored Infantry," Pile wrote in his report, "belongs the honor of first planting their colors on the enemy parapet." The 73rd suffered twenty-seven casualties in the assault, three killed and twenty-four wounded.[27] These would be its last casualties of the war, for on that same day Robert E. Lee surrendered to Ulysses S. Grant at Appomattox in Virginia.

Following the fall of Mobile and the collapse of Confederate resistance from Virginia to Texas, Union troops pushed inland to dismantle what was left of the Confederacy. The 73rd USCT marched to Selma, Alabama, and then returned to Mobile. The regiment then traveled by steamer to Vicksburg, before marching to Jackson, Mississippi, where it spent the month of June.[28] In July, the 73rd returned to New Orleans and bivouacked at Camp Parapet, the place where Brigadier General John W. Phelps had started everything by asking Butler for weapons to arm fugitive slaves.[29]

The 73rd Infantry USCT, originally the 1st Regiment of Butler's Native Guards, was demobilized on September 23, 1865. The white officers, most

25. Report of Colonel F. M. Crandal, 46th USCT, in Woodward, comp., *The Negro in the Military Service of the United States*, 4102 (M-858, roll 3), NA.

26. Quincy to his mother, April 19, 1865, in Quincy *et al.* Papers, LC. The collapse of the Confederacy yielded many opportunities for black troops to demonstrate the ability to use restraint when dealing with their former enemies. "My men have enjoyed the march extremely," Charles Paine wrote from Raleigh, North Carolina, on April 15, 1865. "They know more than one gives them credit for, & they have appreciated their position as conquerors, though they have behaved well" (Charles S. Paine to his father, April 15, 1865, original in possession of Thomas M. Paine, Wellesley, Mass.).

27. *OR*, Vol. XLIX, Pt. 1, pp. 289, 114.

28. During the spring and summer of 1865, the 74th USCT continued its service on Ship Island, while the 75th moved from Morganza to Algiers and eventually to Terrebonne Parish (Field and Staff Muster Roll, May through August, 1865, Compiled Unit Records, 74th and 75th U.S. Col'd Inf., NA).

29. Field and Staff Muster Rolls, April through August, 1865, Compiled Unit Records, 73rd U.S. Col'd Inf., NA; also *OR*, Vol. XLIX, Pt. 2, pp. 512, 845, 984.

of whom had entered the service after Banks's purge of black officers in 1863, were transferred to the 96th USCT. The black enlisted men, whose three-year term of service was about to expire, were mustered out.[30]

To celebrate their discharge from the Union army, 250 veterans from the 1st Regiment of Butler's Native Guards paraded down Conti Street with fife and drums to the office of the New Orleans *Tribune*, the first black daily in the United States and a vocal proponent of black civil rights. On reaching the *Tribune*, the men stopped and gave three cheers. The *Tribune*'s editor acknowledged their salute in the next day's issue. "We take [the] opportunity to assure them that in the full measure of our power, we'll battle with pen in hand, for the same noble cause for which they all suffered, fought and bled; and in whose defense so many of them died in the fray."[31]

The Native Guards had come home, but the world many of these men knew three years earlier when they enlisted was gone. The war was over, and in its place loomed the even more difficult challenge of gaining rights earned on the field of battle.

30. Special Orders No. 67, September 23, 1865, and Wickham Hoffman to Captain A. H. McDonald, October 22, 1865, both in Regimental Papers, U.S. Colored Troops, Box 44, RG 94, AGO, NA. The 74th USCT was mustered out on October 11, the 75th on November 25, 1865 (*Official Army Register*, VIII, 246–51).

31. New Orleans *Tribune*, September 24, 1865.

10

MANHOOD OF THE
COLORED RACE

Military service in the Civil War in-
stilled a great pride among veterans of the Native Guards.[1] Not surprisingly,
this pride translated into the expectation that black civil rights would be
expanded now that the war had ended. This hope was very much in the
minds of several hundred black veterans on October 29, 1865, when they
led a procession down Canal Street and up Baronne to the Friends of Universal Suffrage headquarters.[2] During the rally that followed, speakers eu-
logized the Native Guards for "nobly demonstrating [the] manhood of the
colored race" and encouraged them "to continue in proving their manhood,
by pursuing a course honorable to themselves and their race." Everyone in
the crowd knew what that meant—gaining the right to vote.[3]

1. Blassingame, *Black New Orleans*, 46–47; "Another Victory for Colored Troops," New
Orleans *Black Republican*, April 15, 1865.
2. The Friends of Universal Suffrage was organized in June, 1865, as an alliance between
the all-black Equal Rights League and white Unionists seeking to counter attempts by former
Confederates to regain political power in Louisiana (Charles Vincent, *Black Legislators in Louisiana During Reconstruction* [Baton Rouge, 1976], 38–40).
3. New Orleans *Tribune*, October 31, December 5, 1865. Charles Paine, who had scoffed
at Butler's decision to enlist black troops in 1862, ended the war with a new appreciation of

The drive for black male suffrage had begun in earnest the preceding January with the organization of a local chapter of the National Equal Rights League.[4] One of the driving forces behind the new organization was James H. Ingraham.[5] Born in Mississippi in 1833 to a female slave and a white slave owner, Ingraham was freed by his father at the age of six.[6] When Butler issued his call for black volunteers in 1862, Ingraham helped raise a company and received a lieutenant's commission in the 1st Regiment as a reward.[7] Promoted for bravery at Port Hudson, Ingraham was the next to the last black officer in the 1st Regiment to resign. Once out of the army, Ingraham turned his energy to the burgeoning civil rights movement in New Orleans and became one of its ablest spokesmen. Ingraham was not the only veteran to assume an active role in the Equal Rights League. William B. Barrett, Arnold Bertonneau, Emile Detiége, Robert H. Isabelle, and Ernest Morphy, all former officers in the Native Guards, joined him in the quest for civil rights.[8]

The Equal Rights League faced an uphill battle, for white Louisianians had no intention of giving black men the right to vote. This became evident

the need for black civil rights. "The colored people in some places are stirring the negro suffrage question," he wrote in September, 1865, from New Berne, North Carolina. "I am going to stir them up a little more and let the colored soldier express an opinion. It is a thing that must be done before the South can be trusted to herself & the sooner the better" (Charles J. Paine to his father, September 8, 1865, in Paine Letters [microfilm P-382], MAHS).

4. The National Equal Rights League, which had chapters in many states, was founded in October, 1864, in response to a program of action adopted by the National Convention of Colored Men held in Syracuse, New York (Vincent, *Black Legislators During Reconstruction*, 29).

5. McCrary, *Abraham Lincoln and Reconstruction*, 295; Vincent, *Black Legislators During Reconstruction*, 32; Logsdon and Bell, "Americanization of Black New Orleans," 231–32. Ingraham was elected president of the meeting.

6. Jean-Charles Houzeau, *My Passage at the New Orleans Tribune: A Memoir of the Civil War Era*, ed. David C. Rankin and trans. Gerard F. Denault (Baton Rouge, 1984), 97n; Rankin, "Politics of Caste," 112.

7. List of Officers 1st Regt. Louisiana Native Guard Free Colored, September 26, 1862, in Regimental Papers, U.S. Colored Troops, Box 44, RG 94, AGO, NA.

8. Vincent, *Black Legislators During Reconstruction*, 8, 34–36; New Orleans *Tribune* (French edition), January 10, 1865; Charles Vincent, "Black Louisianians During the Civil War and Reconstruction: Aspects of Their Struggles and Achievements," in *Louisiana's Black Heritage*, ed. Robert R. MacDonald, John R. Kemp, and Edward F. Haas (New Orleans, 1979), 91.

in early 1866, when the state legislature, which consisted primarily of former Confederates, passed a series of restrictive laws designed to reestablish a form of legalized slavery. Alarmed at the rapid deterioration of all they had attempted to accomplish, New Orleans blacks and some radical whites cast about for a strategy that would allow them to gain the vote quickly. Their solution was to reconvene the constitutional convention of 1864 and amend Louisiana's constitution.[9]

Delegates to the convention sympathetic to the plan assembled at the Mechanics Institute in New Orleans on July 30, 1866. After a brief prayer, the group recessed to round up additional members who were too timid or otherwise unwilling to attend. Meanwhile, a procession of black men shouting for civil rights approached Canal Street one-half block from the institute. At the head of the procession were three drummers, a man with a fife, and a man carrying a tattered American flag.[10] Some said it was the flag of the 1st Regiment of the Native Guards.[11] The backbone of the procession consisted of Union army veterans who believed that three years of service entitled them to the right to vote.[12]

As the procession crossed Canal Street, a white man jostled one of the marchers. The black man retorted with a blow, whereupon someone fired a shot. The crowd closed in, and the black drummers beat the "long roll," just as they had during the war to rally the men for battle. The procession pushed on to the Mechanics Institute, where some of its members went inside, taking the flag with them. Outside, the situation worsened as both sides traded insults from a distance. There was a pile of bricks in the street in front of the institute. "We colored men gathered those bricks and defended ourselves as long as the bricks lasted," John Sidney, a former enlisted man in the Native Guards testified, "and the mob closed in on us."[13]

9. *House Reports,* 39th Cong., 2nd Sess. No. 16, p. 3; Eric Foner, *Reconstruction: America's Unfinished Revolution, 1863–1877* (New York, 1988), 262–63; Joe Gray Taylor, *Louisiana Reconstructed, 1863–1877* (Baton Rouge, 1974), 103–105, 125. The Louisiana Constitution of 1864 did not specifically enfranchise black males, although it allowed the state legislature to do so later if it desired.

10. Testimony in *House Reports,* 39th Cong., 2nd Sess., No. 16, p. 77; and *House Executive Documents,* 39th Cong., 2nd Sess., No. 68, pp. 44, 49, 188, 232, 264.

11. Testimony of Charles W. Gibbons, December 25, 1866, in *House Reports,* 39th Cong., 2nd Sess., No. 16, p. 125.

12. Pinchback in the New Orleans *Times,* November 6, 1863.

13. Testimony of Charles W. Gibbons, December 25, 1866, in *House Reports,* 39th Cong., 2nd Sess., No. 16, p. 125; Testimony of John Sidney, January 1, 1866, *ibid.,* 400–401.

The battle lasted two and a half hours. The police were joined by several hundred white men and boys who chased down blacks wherever they encountered them. Charles Gibbons, a former captain in the 3rd Regiment, was walking down the street with a friend when he was accosted by a policeman. "There goes one damned nigger captain, the son of a bitch," the policeman yelled. "Kill him!" Gibbons and his comrade, a veteran of the same regiment, began to run as soon as the officer opened fire. "Let's turn around, and we may have a chance to dodge the balls," Gibbons yelled to his companion. He had used this trick during the war. They had gone about ten steps backward when his friend let out a groan and put a hand to his side. "I am shot," he said, "I am killed." Gibbons turned and ran as fast as he could. He made it as far as the corner of Common and Baronne before he ran into more police, who arrested him and took him to jail.[14]

Arnold Bertonneau also had a close call. Slipping out of the Mechanics Institute, Bertonneau hid behind an oven in an adjacent lot. Eventually the mob found Bertonneau and closed in. Luckily, a policeman came to his aid and protected him, thinking that Bertonneau was white because of his light complexion.[15] Little did the policeman know that the man in his custody was an influential member of the Equal Rights League. One of the original Defenders of the Native Land, later a lieutenant in the Louisiana militia, and eventually a captain in the 2nd Regiment of the Native Guards, Bertonneau was now fighting for black civil rights.

By the time the riot was over, at least 38 persons had been killed and 146 wounded, almost all of them black. Many of the dead were stoned or kicked to death. Others were stabbed or shot. At least 1 of the dead and 9 of the wounded were veterans of the Native Guards.[16]

With congressional elections only three months away, news of the riot enraged voters in the North and strengthened the Radicals in Washington, who captured control of the U.S. Congress.[17] With the Radicals in control,

14. Testimony of Charles W. Gibbons, December 25, 1866, *ibid.*, 125.

15. Testimony of Arnold Bertonneau, August 4, 1866, *House Executive Documents*, 39th Cong., 2nd Sess., No. 68, p. 130; *Official Army Register*, VIII, 248; New Orleans *Tribune*, January 10, 1865.

16. Comparison of the list of casualties in *House Reports,* 39th Cong., 2nd Sess., No. 16, p. 181, with the name index of soldiers serving as USCT (microfilm), NA. The most complete account of the New Orleans riot can be found in Gilles Vandal, *Anatomy of a Tragedy: The New Orleans Riot of 1866* (Lafayette, La., 1986).

17. Foner, *Reconstruction*, 264–71.

Congress passed a series of Reconstruction Acts in 1867 that divided the Southern states into military districts, disfranchised former officers and officials of the Confederacy, and gave black men the right to vote.[18] General Philip Sheridan was named commander of the Fifth Military District, which included Louisiana and Texas. Seeking to make the provisions of the Reconstruction Acts permanent, Sheridan ordered an election for September 27 and 28 to determine whether the state's 1864 constitution should be revised.[19]

White Louisianians boycotted the election, realizing that they would lose now that blacks could vote. As a result, the final vote was overwhelmingly in favor of a new constitution (75,083 for as opposed to 4,006 against). Ninety-eight delegates to the convention, half white and half black, were chosen in the same election.[20] Among the black delegates were six former members of the Native Guards, including Ingraham, Bertonneau, and P. B. S. Pinchback. Louis François, a twenty-seven-year-old black Creole, was also a delegate. One of the youngest members of the convention, François had served during the war as a sergeant in Company B of the 1st Regiment of the Native Guards.[21]

During the convention Ingraham continued to exert the leadership he had exercised as president of the Equal Rights League. Among other items, Ingraham introduced a motion to legalize marriages entered into during slavery. Although this measure did not pass, it was later enacted by the legislature under Pinchback's sponsorship. Pinchback was also active during the constitutional convention and was primarily responsible for the document's civil rights article, which granted blacks the same rights as whites on common carriers and in places of business and entertainment.[22] The new constitution also included provisions authorizing universal desegregated education and giving all adult male citizens the right to vote, regardless of race.[23]

18. It is ironic that the violence of white resistance to black suffrage made certain the very thing whites opposed (Leavens, "*L'Union* and the New Orleans *Tribune*," 68).

19. Taylor, *Louisiana Reconstructed*, 128–32.

20. *Ibid.*, 146–47.

21. Vincent, *Black Legislators During Reconstruction*, 226–27, 52. The other three veterans were Robert H. Isabelle, James Lewis, and Joseph C. Oliver.

22. *Ibid.*, 49, 61–63. Louisiana's equal accommodation law based on this article lasted until 1878, when it was struck down by the United States Supreme Court in *Hall* v. *DeCuir* (Charles A. Lofgren, *The Plessy Case: A Legal-Historical Interpretation* [New York, 1987], 128–31, 185).

23. Taylor, *Louisiana Reconstructed*, 151–53.

The first legislature elected under the provisions of the new constitution reflected the political gains blacks had made. Between 1868 and 1876, more than forty members of the Louisiana House were black, among them five former officers in the Native Guards. Dozens of blacks also served in the Louisiana Senate, four of them veterans of the Native Guards.[24]

One of the most effective legislators was Robert H. Isabelle, a former second lieutenant in the 2nd Regiment.[25] Isabelle believed that educational opportunities for black children could be achieved only with an integrated system of schools. "I want to see the children of the state educated together," he urged from the floor of the House in 1870. "I want to see them play together, to study together, to eat their lunch together; and when they grow up to be men they will love each other, and be ready, if any force comes against the flag of the United States, to take up arms and defend it together."[26] On the Senate side, Pinchback worked for the same goal. Segregated schools, he feared, would cause white children to look on black children as inferiors. Furthermore, Pinchback was convinced that black-only schools would suffer because of a lack of funding and poor teachers. Despite Pinchback's perspicacity, integrated education in New Orleans was short-lived.[27] Arnold Bertonneau sued the city, unsuccessfully, in 1877 for refusing his children admittance to the public schools. Bertonneau's failed suit, in turn, became part of the case law that contributed to the U.S. Supreme

24. Vincent, *Black Legislators During Reconstruction,* 228–38. Members of the House who had served in the Native Guards were William B. Barrett, Edgard C. Davis, Robert H. Isabelle, Ernest Morphy, and Samuel W. Ringgold. The senators were Emile Detiége, Jacques A. Gla, James H. Ingraham, and P. B. S. Pinchback.

25. Isabelle was born to free parents in Opelousas, Louisiana, in 1826. After serving in the legislature, Isabelle earned a law degree from Straight (now Dillard) University and practiced law in New Orleans until his death in 1907 (Charles Vincent, "Robert Hamlin Isabelle," in Glenn R. Conrad, ed., *A Dictionary of Louisiana Biography* [New Orleans, 1988], I, 425).

26. White reaction to Isabelle's remarks was predictable. "It must be evident now to the most incredulous among our population that such a scheme was to be persisted in as the procedure of compelling the white pupils in the public schools to associate with the colored and negro pupils—that such is the fixed determination of the Radicals, and that the time has come when a plain declaration on the part of respectable whites, of all shades of political sentiment, that they will not submit to such an infamous outrage on their rights, should be spoken" (New Orleans *Daily Picayune,* February 9, 1870).

27. Vincent, *Black Legislators During Reconstruction,* 91. Limited racial integration of the public schools began in 1871 but lasted only three years (Louis R. Harlan, "Desegregation in New Orleans Public Schools During Reconstruction," *American Historical Review,* LXVII [1962], 666–68).

Court's adoption of a separate-but-equal doctrine in *Plessy* v. *Ferguson* almost twenty years later.[28]

There was one, albeit minor, civil rights victory in the courts during this period, and it also involved a former member of the Native Guards. Charles S. Sauvenet, the translator in the provost court who helped Butler reorganize the Native Guards and who served throughout the war as an officer in the 2nd Regiment, brought suit against the Bank, a drinking saloon located on Royal Street. Citing the Civil Rights Act of 1869, Sauvenet asked for $10,000 in damages because the proprietors had refused "to furnish him with refreshments because he is a colored person, and ordered him for the same reason to leave their establishment." Judge Henry C. Dibble of the Orleans Parish Eighth District Court found in Sauvenet's favor and awarded him exemplary damages of $1,000.[29]

The fact that Sauvenet was serving as the civil sheriff of Orleans Parish probably helped his case.[30] But Sauvenet was not the only former member of the Native Guards to gain a position of prominence during Reconstruction and use it to his advantage. Francis E. Dumas, the black Creole who had urged his slaves to join the Native Guards in 1862, was almost elected governor of Louisiana.[31] At the 1868 state Republican nominating convention, Dumas received forty-one votes on the first ballot for governor. The runner-

28. Rankin, "The Impact of the Civil War on the Free Colored Community," 400; Lofgren, *Plessy Case*, 136, 238–39 n. 46. See also Otto H. Olsen, *The Thin Disguise: Plessy v. Ferguson, A Documentary Presentation (1864–1896)* (New York, 1967).

29. New Orleans *Daily Picayune*, January 28, 1871; Dale A. Somers, "Black and White in New Orleans: A Study in Urban Race Relations, 1865–1900," *Journal of Southern History*, XL (1974), 27.

30. Several former members of the Native Guards won election or were appointed to municipal posts. James Lewis became the administrator of public improvements in New Orleans (Vincent, *Black Legislators During Reconstruction*, 7). Lewis later assumed a position with the port of New Orleans, attended the National Republican Convention in 1880 as a delegate, and served as surveyor-general of Louisiana in 1884 (Simmons, *Men of Mark*, 957–58). Octave Rey became a captain in the metropolitan police in 1868 and served until 1877. Charles Sauvenet was elected civil sheriff of Orleans Parish in 1870 and served until 1872 (Vincent, *Black Legislators During Reconstruction*, 221).

31. After serving briefly as a captain in the 1st Regiment, Dumas was promoted to major and reassigned to the 2nd Regiment, making him one of only two black field grade officers in the Union army during the Civil War. The other was Major Martin R. Delany of the 104th Infantry, USCT (Glatthaar, *Forged in Battle*, 280).

up in a five-way race was Henry Clay Warmoth, a white Radical from Illinois. Warmoth beat Dumas by two votes in the run-off and went on to defeat the opposition candidate in November by a margin of almost two to one. Warmoth offered Dumas the number two spot on the ticket, but Dumas declined. Oscar J. Dunn, another free man of color before the war, accepted the nomination for lieutenant governor and was elected in Dumas' place.[32]

Although Dumas lost his bid to be governor as a result of Warmoth's ascendancy, another veteran of the Native Guards won. P. B. S. Pinchback was a strong Warmoth supporter and campaigned heavily in 1870 to get out the black vote for Warmoth's second term. As a reward, the Warmoth-controlled legislature named Pinchback lieutenant governor when Dunn died unexpectedly. Pinchback's association with Warmoth did not, however, bring honor to the memory of the Native Guards. Warmoth's administration was corrupt, and Pinchback benefited personally from that corruption. Nevertheless, when Warmoth was removed from office on December 9, 1872, the lieutenant governor became acting governor for the remaining thirty-five days of Warmoth's term. Pinchback thus served as Louisiana's first and only black governor.[33]

Pinchback's brief tenure as acting governor was the political high-water mark for Louisiana blacks during the nineteenth century. Within five years whites had recovered control of Louisiana. By 1898, blacks had lost all the political gains they had achieved, including the right to vote, when the state adopted a new constitution.[34] "For the first time since the war," a white New Orleanian boasted, "we've got the nigger where we want him."[35]

The 1890s were hard years for former members of the Native Guards in

32. Taylor, *Louisiana Reconstructed*, 156–57; Vincent, *Black Legislators During Reconstruction*, 69; Logsdon and Bell, "Americanization of Black New Orleans," 246–50. Carole R. Taylor and Jane B. Chaillot, "Oscar James Dunn," in Glenn R. Conrad, ed., *A Dictionary of Louisiana Biography* (New Orleans, 1988), I, 268–69, state that Dunn had gained a captaincy in the 1st Louisiana Native Guards, but the *Official Army Register* does not list Dunn among the officers of that or any regiment of the Native Guards.

33. Taylor, *Louisiana Reconstructed*, 186, 219–221, 246–47, 253; Agnes Smith Grosz, "The Political Career of Pinckney Benton Stewart Pinchback," *Louisiana Historical Quarterly*, XXVII (1944), 559–603.

34. Anthony, "Negro Creole Community in New Orleans," 44; Foner, *Reconstruction*, 590–96; Taylor, *Louisiana Reconstructed*, 507.

35. R. C. Hitchcock to George Washington Cable, September 1, 1888, quoted in Somers, "Black and White in New Orleans," 42.

other ways as well. Like hundreds of thousands of their white comrades, black veterans organized local chapters (posts) of the powerful veterans' organization the Grand Army of the Republic (GAR). One post was named in honor of André Cailloux, the hero of Port Hudson; another was named for Anselmas Planciancois, flag bearer in the 3rd Regiment, who also lost his life in the assault of May 27.[36]

Although the black veterans did not seek to join white posts, the white Union veterans in Louisiana wanted nothing to do with them. As far as the white veterans were concerned, men who had served in black regiments during the Civil War were not soldiers "in the same sense" as white volunteers. Despite white opposition, the national organization authorized the formation of five black posts in 1889.[37] The matter did not end there, however. The white veterans protested the existence of black posts in their department. Why not set up a "colored department" to handle black veterans who wanted to join the GAR? The GAR's national headquarters said no; black veterans had the right to form their own posts within the organization's existing structure. Refusing to accept this decision, the white leadership of the Department of Louisiana and Mississippi surrendered its charter in 1891. The GAR's commander in chief, Captain John Palmer, responded by appointing a new departmental commander who was more sympathetic to the black veterans. "A man who is willing to stand between the flag and those who would destroy it is good enough to be a comrade in any department of the Grand Army," Palmer declared.[38] Palmer's recognition of the

36. Wilson, *Black Phalanx*, 527–28. Planciancois' first name was also spelled Anselino. Charles Vincent ("Robert Hamlin Isabelle," 425) states that Robert H. Isabelle served as adjutant of the Farragut Post in the GAR but does not indicate whether the post was white or black.

37. Mary R. Dearing, *Veterans in Politics: The Story of the G.A.R.* (Baton Rouge, 1952), 414–15; Stuart McConnell, *Glorious Contentment: The Grand Army of the Republic, 1865–1900* (Chapel Hill, 1992), 216–17.

38. Palmer's speech to the National Encampment in Washington, D.C., printed in the Chicago *Daily Tribune*, September 22, 1892, p. 9. Palmer was irritated by the needless effort the controversy had caused. The discord had "tested the patience, skill, and endurance of my predecessors in their efforts to bring about an amicable adjustment between white and colored posts," Palmer noted in his speech. Trying to resolve it, he declared, "had cost the National Encampment more money, time, and energy . . . than all other departments combined from the inception of this order to the present time."

black posts prompted most of the white members in Louisiana to resign so that by 1898 GAR membership in Louisiana was almost entirely black.[39]

By the turn of the century, most Civil War veterans had reached the age of sixty and were beginning to experience the effects of old age. In 1862 Congress had authorized pensions for Civil War veterans who had suffered injury or disability as a result of their service.[40] Many veterans of the Native Guards came forward to press their cases. Most of their claims were valid. Robert H. Isabelle, for example, landed on the hilt of his sword while jumping from a moving train at Bayou Des Allemands in December, 1862, and suffered a hernia that afflicted him from that point on.[41] Other claims were suspicious, however. Veterans seeking pensions often exaggerated the extent of their disability or attempted to link conditions occurring after their discharge to the hardships of military service. François Hippolyte, for example, who served in both the Louisiana militia and the Native Guards, claimed that "piles [hemorrhoids] and impaired vision" resulted "from straining, long standing and raising heavy guns at Fort McComb while we were in garrison there."[42]

The problem of fraudulent claims was exacerbated by unscrupulous lawyers who collected fees for representing claimants before the pension office.[43] Often these white lawyers induced uneducated black veterans to commit perjury and added to the fraud by having comrades from the same regiment testify that the disability was service-related.[44] The government concluded, for example, that John J. Gage, former sergeant major of the 1st Regiment, had committed both forgery and perjury in submitting his claim. The government's attorney who investigated the case decided that Gage was a "sharp, shrewd, mulatto, while John J. David [the notary who attested to the veracity of Gage's statements] is a white man, and the two are shown to

---

39. Dearing, *Veterans in Politics*, 418.

40. McConnell, *Glorious Contentment*, 143.

41. Pension file for Robert H. Isabelle, NA.

42. Dearing, *Veterans in Politics*, 330–33, 438; Pension file for François Hippolyte, 74th USCT, NA. The government relied on medical examinations performed by competent physicians to validate claims.

43. Dearing, *Veterans in Politics*, 194, 199.

44. For example, see pension file of James Lewis, NA.

have such an influence over the colored people in their community [Fort Adams, Mississippi] that they are completely under their control."[45]

The great majority of the pension claims from former members of the Native Guards were valid.[46] Poor sanitary conditions, the lack of adequate medical attention, and the hardships of service did leave many black veterans completely or partially disabled. At a time before Social Security, these pensions were crucial to the veterans' well-being, even though the amounts were often small (*e.g.*, $8 per month). This was particularly true for the widow who had depended on her husband's income before his death.[47] "I am about seventy-four years of age[,] very broken at that, from dire suffering for want of food, clothes and other requisites of life," wrote a widow whose husband had served in the Native Guards. Concerned because she could not furnish evidence of her age, she wrote, "I humbly beg that you will not let this keep me out of my pension which I so sadly need." The government did not tend to be generous. When Brazil Gardner, a black veteran of the Native Guards, died in 1929, the pension office rejected his widow's claim for a death benefit because the funeral expenses had come to only $28.10 and the pensioner had assets worth $80.[48]

One by one, the Native Guards passed away. Francis E. Dumas died of heart failure on March 27, 1901. His widow lived until 1928. Arnold Bertonneau married a woman twenty-three years his junior in 1891, had four children (he was over sixty), and moved to Pasadena, California. Bertonneau lived there until his death on October 6, 1912. His widow, Julia Lacoste Bertonneau, survived him by more than twenty years. P. B. S. Pinchback also left Louisiana, moved to New York, and eventually ended up in Washington, D.C., where he died on December 21, 1921.[49]

---

45. Chief of Law Division, Department of Interior, Bureau of Pensions, to Chief of the S. E. Division, December 8, 1899, in pension file of John J. Gage, 73rd USCT, NA.

46. For examples, see pension files for Pierre Chevalier, 74th USCT, Louis Levan, 74th USCT, Celicout Sauve, 74th USCT, Orwell Blake, 75th USCT, Philip Pierce, 75th USCT, and Joseph Auguston, 75th USCT, all in NA.

47. For example, see pension files for John Alfred and Louis D. Larriere, both 73rd USCT, NA.

48. Letter dated June 12, 1918, in USCT pension files, NA; pension file for Brazil Gardner, NA.

49. Pension file for Francis E. Dumas, NA; death certificate for Arnold Bertonneau and

Only a handful of the more than three thousand men who had served in either the 1st, 2nd, or 3rd Regiments of the Native Guards lived into the Roaring Twenties. By 1930, only two were left. John H. Hollinger, who had served as a private in the 3rd Regiment, died in New Orleans on July 3, 1932. A cooper by trade, Hollinger was ninety-two when he died. His veteran's death benefit paid for the United States flag on his casket at the funeral.[50] Propher Seream of the same regiment survived his comrade by slightly more than six weeks. Seream died in New Orleans on August 19, 1932.[51]

It was over. There was no one left to tell the story of the Native Guards. World War II came and went, and with it the hopes of black veterans for an equal place in the American dream. So it was following Korea and Vietnam. The hopes and aspirations were not new. It had all happened before, and the Native Guards had been the first. But even they could not have envisioned in April, 1861, where what they started would end. From their Confederate origins to their Reconstruction activism, these men asked to be accepted as responsible citizens of the state they loved. At every turn, however, they were rebuffed. The Confederate authorities used their service to counter Northern propaganda but never intended to let them fight. The Union army let them fight but made them dig ditches when their capacity for fighting became evident. After the war, whites accepted them for their labor but

affidavit dated October 16, 1931, attached to his widow's declaration of September 30, 1930, all in Bertonneau's pension file, NA; Grosz, "Political Career of Pinchback," 606–607; also Pinchback's pension file, NA. Pinchback served in the 1879 constitutional convention and was successful in getting a provision to establish a state-supported "university for the education of persons of color." In 1880 the legislature made the provision a reality when it established Southern University. Pinchback served as a member on Southern's Board of Trustees in 1883 and 1885.

50. Hollinger was born on October 25, 1840 (pension file for John H. Hollinger, 75th USCT, NA). Many of the pension index cards do not give a date of death for the pensioner. Therefore, it is possible that other veterans of the Native Guards lived longer than either Hollinger or Seream. Because veterans surviving into the mid-1930s would have been in their nineties, however, it is not unreasonable to assume that Hollinger and Seream were among the last, if not the last, veterans of the Native Guards to die.

51. General Pension Index (T-289) for 73rd, 74th, and 75th Infantry, USCT, rolls 559 and 560, NA. The last black soldier in the Civil War died on July 15, 1951. His name was Joseph Clovese (Gladstone, *Men of Color*, 180).

repudiated their quest for equal rights. Pawns of three governments, the men of the Native Guards worked hard and did their duty, but as Lieutenant Colonel Quincy observed when he wrote to his mother from Port Hudson in April, 1864, "Nobody really desires our success[,] and it is uphill work."[52]

52. Quincy to his mother, April 25, 1864, in Quincy *et al.* Papers, LC.

BLACK OFFICERS
IN THE NATIVE
GUARDS

Several attempts have been made to identify the black officers who served in the Native Guards. This task is not as easy as it might appear. The service records of Civil War soldiers normally do not contain information regarding race. Although reference to an officer's race may appear occasionally in a letter of resignation or other correspondence, generally one must infer whether an officer is black on the basis of other information.

It is generally accepted that all of the line officers in the 1st and 2nd Regiments were black when the two units were mustered into the Union army on September 27 and October 12, 1862, respectively.[1] Furthermore, it is unlikely that additional black officers were commissioned after these dates. Nathaniel P. Banks superseded Butler on December 9, 1862, and Banks had no intention of adding to the ranks of commissioned blacks. The situation

1. Berry, "Negro Troops in Blue and Gray," 175. The muster-in roll for the 2nd Regiment lists a free man of color, Samuel Lawrence, as second lieutenant of Company A, but Lawrence was replaced by William S. Peabody, who volunteered from the ranks of the 8th Vermont Infantry. Peabody thus became the first white line officer of a black regiment (Peabody's Compiled Military Service Record, NA). Lawrence was commissioned as a captain in the 3rd Regiment when it was mustered in a month later.

in the 3rd Regiment is less clear because this regiment contained both black and white officers when it was organized. Because all of the black officers in the 3rd Regiment resigned en masse on February 19, 1863, their identity can be determined from the list of names included in the letter of resignation.

The first attempt to identify the black officers in the Native Guards was made in 1888, when Joseph T. Wilson published his compilation of sixty-six names on page 176 of *The Black Phalanx*. A second list of seventy-three names was prepared by the editors of *Freedom: A Documentary History of Emancipation, 1861–1867* and appeared in 1982 as a footnote on pages 310–11 in the second volume, *The Black Military Experience*. Joseph T. Glatthaar reprinted the *Freedom* list with three additions and one deletion in 1990 as an appendix to *Forged in Battle*.[2]

There are several problems with the previous lists. They do not agree with each other, and all three include errors of unit affiliation.[3] All three lists fail to include the names of several black officers who did serve, and they identify several white officers as being black.[4]

Below is my list of seventy-six black officers in the Native Guards. It comes from the roster of all the line officers in the 1st and 2nd Regiments of the Native Guards taken directly from company muster rolls on the day each regiment was mustered into service. For the 3rd Regiment, I used the names of the sixteen black officers who resigned in February, 1863.

A comparison of my list with the lists of Wilson and Glatthaar revealed that there were nine names on Wilson's list (five of these were also on Glatthaar's list) that do not appear on mine. I examined the compiled military service records for these nine individuals and found that seven were white Union soldiers from Northern states who had volunteered to serve as officers

2. Glatthaar added the names of John Crowder, Edgard Davis, and Joseph Montieu, all of the 1st Regiment. He deleted the name of Rufus Kinsley, a white officer who served in the 2nd Regiment.

3. The correct unit affiliation can be determined from the *Official Army Register*, which corresponds to the affiliations recorded in the individual compiled military service records in the National Archives.

4. For example, Lieutenant G. B. Miller appears on both the Wilson and Glatthaar lists as a black officer in the 3rd Regiment, whereas the *Official Army Register* indicates that Greenleaf B. Miller of the 75th USCT died of disease on March 1, 1867, while stationed at Brazos Springs, Texas. I am not aware of any evidence to suggest that black officers served in the U.S. Army during Reconstruction.

in the Native Guards. I could find no record for one man, John Hardman, although his name appears in Wilson's list as serving in the 1st Regiment. The ninth man, E. T. Nash, is in the *Official Army Register,* but my request for his compiled military service record resulted in a rejection slip. Because Nash's name does not appear on any of the original muster rolls, I assume that he was white.

BLACK OFFICERS IN THE NATIVE GUARDS*

NAME/COMMENTS	RANK	RESIGNED	WILSON	GLATTHAAR
1st Regiment				
Bourgeau, Alfred Promoted in October, 1863	1LT	3/07/64	3rd	1st
Butler, Charles Medical discharge, rheumatism	2LT	4/04/63	3rd	3rd
Cailloux, Andrew Killed at Port Hudson	CPT	5/27/63	1st	1st
Carter, Edward Medical discharge, piles	CPT	10/21/63	1st	1st
Case, George R. Medical discharge, deafness	CPT	2/11/64		
Crowder, John Killed at Port Hudson	2LT	5/27/63		1st
Davis, Edgard Transferred to 91st USCT and resigned	CPT	9/01/63		1st
Depass, John Resigned to return to England	CPT	2/27/63	1st	1st
Detiége, Emile Resigned for reasons of prejudice	1LT	9/25/63	3rd	1st
Follin, Joseph Resigned for reasons of prejudice	CPT	2/29/64	1st	1st

*Spelling of names, rank, and unit affiliation come from the *Official Army Register*, VIII, 246–251. Unit affiliation according to the *Official Army Register* for the white officers misidentified as black is indicated in parentheses.

NAME/COMMENTS	RANK	RESIGNED	WILSON	GLATTHAAR
Fog[y], Octave Discharged for physical disability	2LT	3/30/63	3rd	3rd
Ingraham, James H. Promoted in October, 1863	CPT	3/22/64	1st	1st
Laniez, Louis D. Resigned but no service record	1LT	6/03/63	1st	1st
Lavigne, Victor Transferred to 91st USCT and resigned	2LT	9/05/63		1st
Lewis, Alcide Dismissed for cowardice	CPT	8/26/63	1st	1st
Lewis, James Medical discharge, piles	CPT	3/14/64	1st	1st
Mallet, Jules Transferred to 91st USCT and resigned	1LT	9/05/63		1st
Montieu, Joseph L. Transferred to 91st USCT and resigned	2LT	9/01/63		1st
Morris, Morris W. Resigned on death of father	1LT	8/27/63	3rd	1st
Moss, Ehurd Resigned to avoid being discharged	1LT	3/14/64	3rd	1st
Orillion, Oscar Missing in action near Jackson, Louisiana	2LT	8/03/63		1st
Paree, Paul Medical discharge, rheumatism	1LT	8/11/63	3rd	1st
Rapp, Eugene Resigned, no reason given	1LT	9/27/63	3rd	1st
Rey, Henry L. Medical discharge, disease	CPT	4/06/63	1st	1st
Sentmanat, Charles Transferred to 91st USCT and resigned	CPT	10/02/63		1st

NAME/COMMENTS	RANK	RESIGNED	WILSON	GLATTHAAR
Snaer, Louis A. On duty at the end of the war	CPT	11/27/65	1st	
St. Louis, Hyppolite Dismissed by Banks	2LT	8/26/63		1st
Thibaut, Louis A. Dismissed by Banks	2LT	8/26/63		1st
Warfield, Charles Resigned, benefit of the service	2LT	2/27/63		1st

2nd Regiment

NAME/COMMENTS	RANK	RESIGNED	WILSON	GLATTHAAR
Barrett, William B. Resigned for reasons of prejudice	CPT	7/20/63	2nd	2nd
Belley, William Resigned, not qualified by examining board	CPT	4/05/64	2nd	2nd
Bertonneau, Arnold Resigned for reasons of prejudice	CPT	3/05/63	2nd	2nd
Carter, Hannibal Resigned, Special Orders No. 126	CPT	5/30/63	2nd	2nd
Chase, Edward P. Resigned, Special Orders No. 126	CPT	5/30/63	2nd	2nd
De Gray, Louis Resigned, Special Orders No. 126	1LT	5/30/63	2nd	2nd
Depremont, Peter O. Resigned, no reason given	2LT	7/17/63	2nd	2nd
Dumas, Francis E. Resigned, no reason given	MAJ	7/03/63	2nd	2nd
Fleury, Alphonse, Jr. Medical discharge, sickness	1LT	4/04/63	2nd	2nd
Glover, Calvin B. Resigned, Special Orders No. 126	1LT	5/30/63	2nd	2nd
Hays, Solomon "Ignorant, unable to learn"	2LT	2/18/64	2nd	2nd

NAME/COMMENTS	RANK	RESIGNED	WILSON	GLATTHAAR
Hubeau, Ernest Resigned, no reason	1LT	1/22/63	2nd	2nd
Isabelle, Robert H. Resigned for reasons of prejudice	2LT	3/05/63	2nd	2nd
Jones, Joseph Resigned, no reason given	1LT	7/13/63	2nd	2nd
Keeling, William F. Dismissed by board, Special Orders No. 55	1LT	2/24/63		
Latting, John W. Resigned, Special Orders No. 126	2LT	5/30/63		2nd
Louis, Jules P. Medical discharge, sickness	2LT	4/04/63	2nd	2nd
Martin, Theodule A. Medical discharge, scurvy	1LT	8/15/64	2nd	2nd
Merillion, Monroe Dismissed by board, Special Orders No. 55	CPT	2/24/63	2nd	
Morphy, Ernest Resigned for reasons of prejudice	1LT	3/05/63	2nd	2nd
Pinchback, P. B. S. "Only col'd officer" at Fort Pike	CPT	9/11/63	2nd	2nd
Rey, Octave Resigned for reasons of prejudice	2LT	3/05/63	2nd	2nd
Ringgold, Samuel W. Protested makeup of examining board	CPT	7/20/63	2nd	2nd
Sauvenet, Charles S. Promoted to assistant quartermaster	1LT	7/11/65		
Scott, Lucien Dismissed by board, Special Orders No. 55	2LT	2/24/63		
Thompson, Jasper Resigned, Special Orders No. 126	2LT	5/30/63	2nd	2nd

NAME/COMMENTS	RANK	RESIGNED	WILSON	GLATTHAAR
Trask, Frank L. Dismissed, left guard post	2LT	2/21/64		2nd
Villeverde, Joseph Dismissed by board, Special Orders No. 215	CPT	8/15/64	2nd	2nd
Watson, George F. Resigned, Special Orders No. 126	1LT	5/30/63	2nd	2nd
Wellington, Joseph Resigned, Special Orders No. 126	1LT	5/30/63	2nd	2nd
Wilkinson, Samuel J. Protested makeup of examining board	CPT	7/20/63	2nd	2nd

3rd Regiment

NAME/COMMENTS	RANK	RESIGNED	WILSON	GLATTHAAR
Forstall, Leon G. Mass resignation	CPT	2/19/63	3rd	3rd
Gardiner, Peter A. Mass resignation	CPT	2/19/63	3rd	3rd
Gibbons, Charles W. Mass resignation	CPT	2/19/63	3rd	3rd
Gla, Jacques Adolph Mass resignation	CPT	2/19/63	3rd	3rd
Hardin, William Mass resignation	2LT	2/19/63	1st	3rd
Holland, John C. Mass resignation	CPT	2/19/63	3rd	3rd
Lawrence, Samuel Mass resignation	CPT	2/19/63	3rd	3rd
Lesassier, Valdes Mass resignation	2LT	2/19/63	1st	3rd
Longpre, Ernest Mass resignation	1LT	2/19/63	1st	3rd
Moore, James E. Mass resignation	2LT	2/19/63	1st	3rd

NAME/COMMENTS	RANK	RESIGNED	WILSON	GLATTHAAR
Oliver, Joseph C. Mass resignation, "excellent officer"	CPT	2/19/63	3rd	3rd
Parker, Joseph G. Mass resignation	2LT	2/19/63	1st	3rd
Petit, Louis Mass resignation	1LT	2/19/63	1st	3rd
Rey, Hippolyte Mass resignation	2LT	2/19/63		3rd
Schermerhorn, Charles Mass resignation	2LT	2/19/63		3rd
Tervalon, Francois Mass resignation	1LT	2/19/63		3rd

White Officers Misidentified as Black

NAME/COMMENTS	RANK	RESIGNED	WILSON	GLATTHAAR
Annis, Alfred (2nd) Transferred from 91st USCT	2LT	7/18/65	2nd	2nd
Converse, Chester (1st) Resigned to return to the North	1LT	5/28/64	3rd	3rd
Hardman, John (?) No record	?	?	1st	
Kimball, Frank (3rd) Commissioned on 1/09/64	1LT	11/21/64	1st	
Kinsley, Rufus (2nd) From Boston, medical discharge	2LT	7/18/65	2nd	
Miller, Greenleaf (1st) Died on duty in Texas, 1867	1LT	11/24/64	3rd	3rd
Nash, E. T. (1st) Rejection slip	1LT	10/16/63	3rd	3rd
Paddock, John D. (3rd) From Massachusetts	2LT	12/06/64	1st	
Tallmon, George (1st) Transferred from 20th Iowa	1LT	5/03/65	3rd	3rd

BIBLIOGRAPHY

MANUSCRIPT COLLECTIONS

Historic New Orleans Collection, New Orleans, Louisiana.
    Bennett, Charles. Letters.
    Townsend Letter, MS 280.
Howard-Tilton Memorial Library, Tulane University, New Orleans, Louisiana.
    Civil War Letters, 1862–63, Civil War Manuscripts Series.
    Louisiana Historical Association Collection.
Louisiana and Lower Mississippi Valley Collections, LSU Libraries, Louisiana State
    University, Baton Rouge, Louisiana.
    Andrews, George L. Papers.
    Fessenden, Anson D. Papers.
    Guild, John H. Letters.
    Johnston, Henry. Letter.
    Slauson, D[aniel] D. Papers.
    Wharton, E. C. Family Letters.
    Yawyer, Peter M. Letters.
Library of Congress, Washington, D.C.
    Banks, Nathaniel P. Collection.
    Quincy, Wendell, Holmes, and Upham Family Papers.
Massachusetts Historical Society, Boston, Massachusetts.
    Dame, Lorin L. Diary.
    Dwight Family Papers.
    Eastman, William H. Letters.
    Miller, James. Diary.
    Paine, Charles J. Letters. Microfilm.
Minnesota Historical Society, Saint Paul, Minnesota.
    Babcock, Willoughby, and Family Papers.
National Archives, Washington, D.C.
    American Freedmen's Inquiry Commission Report, M-619, roll 200.
    Compiled Military Service Records, Civil War.

Compiled Records Showing Service of Military Units in Volunteer Union Organizations, M-594.

Pension Files, Civil War.

Records of the Louisiana State Government, 1850–88, in War Department Collection of Confederate Records, M-359.

Records of the U.S. Army Continental Command, Letters Received, Department of the Gulf, Record Group 393.

Regimental Books, Civil War, Record Group 94, Adjutant General's Office.

Regimental Papers, U.S. Colored Troops, Record Group 94, Adjutant General's Office.

Smith, William F., and James T. Brady. "Commission on Corrupt Practices in the South, Final Report, Sept. 23, 1865," Record Group 94, Adjutant General's Office.

Woodward, Elon A., comp. *The Negro in the Military Service of the United States, 1639–1886: A Compilation,* M-858.

National Park Service, Technical Information Center, Denver, Colorado.

Bearss, Edwin C. *Historic Resource Study, Ship Island, Harrison County, Mississippi: Gulf Islands National Seashore, Florida/Mississippi.*

New Orleans Public Library, New Orleans, Louisiana.

Muster rolls for the Native Guards, Louisiana Troops.

New-York Historical Society, New York, New York.

Misc. Mss. Wilkinson, R. F.

Ullmann, Daniel. Papers.

United States Military History Institute, Carlisle Barracks, Pennsylvania.

Hughes, Robert. Papers.

Vermont Historical Society, Montpelier, Vermont.

Kinsley, Rufus. Diary.

Yale University, New Haven, Connecticut.

Civil War Miscellaneous Collection.

GOVERNMENT DOCUMENTS

Congressional Record, 44th Cong., 1st Sess.

House Executive Documents, 39th Cong., 2nd Sess. No. 68.

House Reports, 39th Cong., 2nd Sess. No. 16.

Official Army Register of the Volunteer Force of the United States Army for the Year 1861, '62, '63, '64, '65. 1865; rpr., 10 vols. Gaithersburg, Md., 1987.

Official Records of the Union and Confederate Navies in the War of the Rebellion. 30 vols.; Washington, D.C., 1894–1927.

Report of the Joint Committee on the Conduct of the War, at the Second Session Thirty-Eighth Congress, vol. 2, *Red River Campaign.* Washington, D.C., 1865.
Senate Reports, 37th Cong., 3rd Sess., No. 108.
The War of the Rebellion: A Compilation of the Official Records of the Union and Confederate Armies. 70 vols. in 127 and index. Washington, D.C., 1880–1901.

NEWSPAPERS

Boston *Daily Evening Transcript,* 1863.
Charleston *Mercury,* 1863.
Chicago *Daily Tribune,* 1863, 1892.
Douglass Monthly, 1863.
Harper's Weekly, 1863.
Liberator, 1862, 1864.
National Anti-Slavery Standard, 1862–63.
National Intelligencer, 1863.
New Orleans *Black Republican,* 1865.
New Orleans *Daily Crescent,* 1861.
New Orleans *Daily Delta,* 1860, 1862.
New Orleans *Daily Picayune,* 1859, 1861–63, 1865, 1870–71.
New Orleans *Daily True Delta,* 1861–63.
New Orleans *Republican,* 1867.
New Orleans *Times,* 1863.
New Orleans *Times Democrat,* 1906.
New Orleans *Tribune,* 1864–65.
New Orleans *L'Union,* 1862–63.
New Orleans *Weekly Louisianian,* 1875.
New York *Daily Tribune,* 1863–64.
New York *Herald,* 1863.
New York *Times,* 1862–64.

THESES AND DISSERTATIONS

Anthony, Arthé Agnes. "The Negro Creole Community in New Orleans, 1880–1920: An Oral History." Ph.D. dissertation, University of California, Irvine, 1978.
Everett, Donald E. "Free Persons of Color in New Orleans, 1803–1865." Ph.D. dissertation, Tulane University, 1952.
Leavens, Finian P. *"L'Union* and the New Orleans *Tribune* and Louisiana Reconstruction." M.A. thesis, Louisiana State University, 1966.

Leland, Edwin Albert. "Organization and Administration of the Louisiana Army During the Civil War." M.S. thesis, Louisiana State University, 1938.

Messner, William F. "The Federal Army and Blacks in the Department of the Gulf, 1862–1865." Ph.D. dissertation, University of Wisconsin, 1972.

Rankin, David C. "The Forgotten People: Free People of Color in New Orleans, 1850–1870." Ph.D. dissertation, Johns Hopkins University, 1976.

ARTICLES, PAMPHLETS, AND CHAPTERS

Berry, Mary F. "Negro Troops in Blue and Gray: The Louisiana Native Guards, 1861–1863." *Louisiana History*, VIII (1967), 165–90.

Blassingame, John W. "The Selection of Officers and Non-Commissioned Officers of Negro Troops in the Union Army, 1863–1865." *Negro History Bulletin*, XXX (1967), 8–12.

————. "The Union Army as an Educational Institution for Negroes, 1862–1865." *Journal of Negro Education*, XXXIV (1965), 152–59.

Bryant, William Cullen, ed. "A Yankee Soldier Looks at the Negro." *Civil War History*, VII (June, 1961), 133–48.

Chase, Salmon P. "Diary and Correspondence of Salmon P. Chase." In *Annual Report of the American Historical Association; The Year 1902*. 16 vols. in 24 parts. Washington, D.C., 1903.

Dargan, James F. *My Experiences in Service, or a Nine Months Man*. American Classics Facsimile Series, edited by Norman Tanis. Los Angeles, 1974.

Dunbar-Nelson, Alice. "People of Color in Louisiana, Part II." *Journal of Negro History*, II (1917), 51–78.

Everett, Donald E. "Ben Butler and the Louisiana Native Guards, 1861–1862." *Journal of Southern History*, XXIV (1958), 201–17.

Fitts, James Franklin. "The Negro in Blue." *Galaxy*, III (1867), 249–55.

Frederick, J. V., ed. "War Diary of W. C. Porter." *Arkansas Historical Quarterly*, XI (1952), 286–314.

Glatthaar, Joseph T. "The Civil War Through the Eyes of a Sixteen-Year-Old Black Officer: The Letters of Lieutenant John H. Crowder of the 1st Louisiana Native Guards." *Louisiana History*, XXXV (1994), 201–16.

Grosz, Agnes Smith. "The Political Career of Pinckney Benton Stewart Pinchback." *Louisiana Historical Quarterly*, XXVII (1944), 559–603.

Harlan, Louis R. "Desegregation in New Orleans Public Schools During Reconstruction." *American Historical Review*, LXVII (1962), 663–75.

Hawes, Levi Lindley. "Personal Experiences of a Union Veteran." *Historic Leaves*, IV (October, 1905), 49–62.

Jackson, Crawford M. "An Account of the Occupation of Fort Hudson." *Alabama Historical Quarterly*, XVIII (1956), 474–85.

Jackson, Joy J. "Samuel Miller Quincy." In vol. II of *A Dictionary of Louisiana Biography*, edited by Glenn R. Conrad. New Orleans, 1988.

James, Felix. "Andre Callioux [*sic*]." In vol. I of *A Dictionary of Louisiana Biography*, edited by Glenn R. Conrad. New Orleans, 1988.

Joshi, Manoj K., and Joseph P. Reidy. "'To Come Forward and Aid in Putting Down This Unholy Rebellion': The Officers of Louisiana's Free Black Native Guard During the Civil War Era." *Southern Studies*, XXI (1982), 326–42.

Logsdon, Joseph, and Caryn Cossé Bell. "The Americanization of Black New Orleans, 1850–1900." In *Creole New Orleans: Race and Americanization*, edited by Arnold R. Hirsch and Joseph Logsdon. Baton Rouge, 1992.

McConnell, Roland C. "Louisiana's Black Military History." In *Louisiana's Black Heritage*, edited by Robert R. MacDonald, John R. Kemp, and Edward F. Haas. New Orleans, 1979.

Moore, David W. "Armand Lanusse." In vol. I of *A Dictionary of Louisiana Biography*, edited by Glenn R. Conrad. New Orleans, 1988.

Palfrey, John C. "Port Hudson." In *The Mississippi Valley, Tennessee, Georgia, Alabama, 1861–1864*. Vol. VIII of the *Papers of the Military Historical Society of Massachusetts*. Boston, 1910.

Quincy, Samuel M. *A Camp and Garrison Manual for Volunteers and Militia*. New Orleans, 1865.

Rankin, David C. "The Impact of the Civil War on the Free Colored Community of New Orleans." In vol. XI of *Perspectives in American History*, edited by Donald Fleming. Cambridge, Mass., 1978.

———. "The Politics of Caste: Free Colored Leadership in New Orleans During the Civil War." In *Louisiana's Black Heritage*, edited by Robert R. MacDonald, John R. Kemp, and Edward F. Haas. New Orleans, 1979.

Root, William H. "The Experiences of a Federal Soldier in Louisiana in 1863." Edited by L. Carroll Root. *Louisiana Historical Quarterly*, XIX (1936), 635–67.

Roy, Joseph E. "Our Indebtedness to the Negroes for Their Conduct During the War." *New Englander and Yale Review*, LI (1889), 353–64.

Schoonover, Thomas D. "Francis Ernest Dumas." In vol. I of *A Dictionary of Louisiana Biography*, edited by Glenn R. Conrad. New Orleans, 1988.

Shewmaker, Kenneth, and Andrew Prinz, eds. "A Yankee in Louisiana: Selections from the Diary and Correspondence of Henry R. Gardner, 1862–1866." *Louisiana History*, V (1964), 271–95.

Smith, M. J., and James Freret. "Fortification and Siege of Port Hudson." *Southern Historical Society Papers*, XIV (1886), 305–48.

Somers, Dale A. "Black and White in New Orleans: A Study in Urban Race Relations, 1865–1900." *Journal of Southern History*, XL (1974), 19–42.

Taylor, Carole R., and Jane B. Chaillot. "Oscar James Dunn." In vol. I of *A Dictionary of Louisiana Biography*, edited by Glenn R. Conrad. New Orleans, 1988.

Vincent, Charles. "Black Louisianians During the Civil War and Reconstruction: Aspects of Their Struggles and Achievements." In *Louisiana's Black Heritage*, edited by Robert R. MacDonald, John R. Kemp, and Edward F. Haas. New Orleans, 1979.

———. "Robert Hamlin Isabelle." In vol. I of *A Dictionary of Louisiana Biography*, edited by Glenn R. Conrad. New Orleans, 1988.

War Record of Col.? W. M. Grosvenor, Editor of the Missouri Democrat. N.p., n.d., copy in New York Public Library.

Wesley, Charles H. "The Employment of Negroes as Soldiers in the Confederate Army." *Journal of Negro History*, IV (1919), 239–53.

Williams, Walter. "William Mason Grosvenor." In *Dictionary of American Biography*, vol. VIII, 26–27. New York, 1935.

Wright, Howard C. *Port Hudson: Its History from an Interior Point of View as Sketched from the Diary of an Officer.* 1937; rpr. Baton Rouge, 1961.

BOOKS

Babcock, Willoughby M., Jr., ed. *Selections from the Letters and Diaries of Brevet-Brigadier General Willoughby Babcock of the Seventy-fifth New York Volunteers.* Albany, 1922.

Bacon, Edward. *Among the Cotton Thieves.* 1867; rpr. Bossier City, La., 1989.

Bartlett, Napier. *Military Record of Louisiana: Including Biographical and Historical Papers Relating to the Military Organizations of the State.* New Orleans, 1875.

Beecher, Harris H. *Record of the 114th Regiment, N.Y. S.V., Where It Went, What It Saw, and What It Did.* Norwich, N.Y., 1866.

Bergeron, Arthur W., Jr., ed. *The Civil War Reminiscences of Major Silas T. Grisamore, C.S.A.* Baton Rouge, 1993.

Berlin, Ira, *et al.*, eds. *Freedom: A Documentary History of Emancipation, 1861–1867.* Ser. I, *The Destruction of Slavery.* New York, 1985. Ser. II, *The Black Military Experience.* New York, 1982.

Blassingame, John W. *Black New Orleans, 1860–1880.* Chicago, 1973.

Booth, Andrew B. *Records of Louisiana Confederate Soldiers and Louisiana Confederate Commands.* 3 vols. 1920; rpr. Spartanburg, S.C., 1984.

Bosson, Charles P. *History of the Forty-second Regiment Infantry, Massachusetts Volunteers, 1862, 1863, 1864.* Boston, 1886.

Brown, William Wells. *The Negro in the American Rebellion: His Heroism and His Fidelity.* 1867; rpr. New York, 1968.

Butler, Benjamin Franklin. *Butler's Book: Autobiography and Personal Reminiscences of Major-General Benj. F. Butler.* Boston, 1892.

————. *Private and Official Correspondence of Gen. Benjamin F. Butler During a Period of the Civil War.* Edited by Jessie Ames Marshall. 5 vols. Norwood, Mass., 1917.

Carpenter, George N. *History of the Eighth Regiment Vermont Volunteers, 1861–1865.* Boston, 1886.

Casey, Powell A. *Encyclopedia of Forts, Posts, Named Camps, and Other Military Installations in Louisiana, 1700–1981.* Baton Rouge, 1983.

Caughey, John Walton. *Bernardo de Gálvez in Louisiana, 1776–1783.* 1934; rpr. Gretna, La., 1972.

Cornish, Dudley Taylor. *The Sable Arm: Negro Troops in the Union Army, 1861–1865.* New York, 1966.

Corsan, W. C. *Two Months in the Confederate States.* 1863; rpr. Baton Rouge, forthcoming.

Crute, Joseph H. *Confederate Staff Officers, 1861–1865.* Powhatan, Va., 1982.

Cunningham, Edward. *The Port Hudson Campaign, 1862–1863.* Baton Rouge, 1963.

Dearing, Mary R. *Veterans in Politics: The Story of the G.A.R.* Baton Rouge, 1952.

De Forest, John William. *A Volunteer's Adventures: A Union Captain's Record of the Civil War.* Edited by James H. Croushore. New Haven, 1946.

Desdunes, Rodolphe Lucien. *Our People and Our History.* Translated and edited by Sister Dorothea Olga McCants. Baton Rouge, 1973.

Dufour, Charles L. *The Night the War Was Lost.* Garden City, N.Y., 1960.

Edmonds, David C. *The Guns of Port Hudson.* Vol. 2, *The Investment, Siege and Reduction.* Lafayette, La., 1984.

Flinn, Frank M. *Campaigning with Banks in Louisiana, '63 and '64, and with Sheridan in the Shenandoah Valley in '64 and '65.* Lynn, Mass., 1887.

Foner, Eric. *Reconstruction: America's Unfinished Revolution, 1863–1877.* New York, 1988.

Fox, William F. *Regimental Losses in the American Civil War, 1861–1865.* Albany, 1889.

Gardner, Charles. *Gardner's New Orleans Directory for 1861.* New Orleans, 1861.

Garvey, John B., and Mary Lou Widmer. *Beautiful Crescent: A History of New Orleans.* New Orleans, 1982.

Gerteis, Louis S. *From Contraband to Freedman: Federal Policy Toward Southern Blacks, 1861–1865.* Westport, Conn., 1973.

Gladstone, William A. *Men of Color*. Gettysburg, Pa., 1993.

———. *United States Colored Troops, 1863–1867*. Gettysburg, Pa., 1990.

Glatthaar, Joseph T. *Forged in Battle: The Civil War Alliance of Black Soldiers and White Officers*. New York, 1990.

Harrington, Fred Harvey. *Fighting Politician: Major General N. P. Banks*. Philadelphia, 1948.

Hepworth, George H. *The Whip, Hoe and Sword; or, The Gulf-Department in '63*. Boston, 1864.

Hewitt, Lawrence Lee. *Port Hudson, Confederate Bastion on the Mississippi*. Baton Rouge, 1987.

Hirsch, Arnold R., and Joseph Logsdon. *Creole New Orleans: Race and Americanization*. Baton Rouge, 1992.

Houzeau, Jean-Charles. *My Passage at the New Orleans* Tribune: *A Memoir of the Civil War Era*. Edited by David C. Rankin and translated by Gerard F. Denault. Baton Rouge, 1984.

Hunt, Roger D., and Jack R. Brown. *Brevet Brigadier Generals in Blue*. Gaithersburg, Md., 1990.

Irwin, Richard B. *History of the Nineteenth Army Corps*. 1892; rpr. Baton Rouge, 1985.

Jimerson, Randall C. *The Private Civil War: Popular Thought During the Sectional Conflict*. Baton Rouge, 1988.

Johns, Henry T. *Life with the Forty-ninth Massachusetts Volunteers*. Pittsfield, Mass., 1864.

Johnson, Ludwell H. *Red River Campaign: Politics and Cotton in the Civil War*. 1958; rpr. Gaithersburg, Md., 1986.

Leslie's Illustrated Civil War. 1894; rpr. Jackson: University Press of Mississippi, 1992.

Lofgren, Charles A. *The Plessy Case: A Legal-Historical Interpretation*. New York, 1987.

McConnell, Roland C. *Negro Troops of Antebellum Louisiana: A History of the Battalion of Free Men of Color*. Baton Rouge, 1968.

McConnell, Stuart. *Glorious Contentment: The Grand Army of the Republic, 1865–1900*. Chapel Hill, 1992.

McCrary, Peyton. *Abraham Lincoln and Reconstruction: The Louisiana Experiment*. Princeton, 1978.

McMorries, Edward Young. *History of the First Regiment, Alabama Volunteer Infantry, C.S.A.* Publication of the State of Alabama Department of Archives and History, no. 2. Montgomery, 1904.

Moors, J. F. *History of the Fifty-second Regiment of Massachusetts Volunteers*. Boston, 1893.

Nell, William C. *The Colored Patriots of the American Revolution*. Boston, 1855.

Olsen, Otto H. *The Thin Disguise: Plessy v. Ferguson, A Documentary Presentation (1864–1896)*. New York, 1967.

Parton, James. *General Butler in New Orleans: History of the Administration of the Department of the Gulf in the Year 1862*. New York, 1864.

Phillips, Ulrich Bonnell. *American Negro Slavery: A Survey of the Supply, Employment and Control of Negro Labor as Determined by the Plantation Regime*. 1918; rpr. Baton Rouge, 1966.

Quarles, Benjamin. *The Negro in the Civil War*. Boston, 1953.

Raphael, Morris. *The Battle in the Bayou Country*. Detroit, 1976.

Redkey, Edwin S., ed. *A Grand Army of Black Men: Letters from African-American Soldiers in the Union Army, 1861–1865*. New York, 1992.

Reinders, Robert C. *End of an Era: New Orleans, 1850–1860*. New Orleans, 1964.

Ripley, Charles P. *Slaves and Freedmen in Civil War Louisiana*. Baton Rouge, 1976.

Robertson, John. *Michigan in the War*. Lansing, Mich., 1882.

Rouse, E. S. S. *The Bugle Blast: or, Spirit of the Conflict*. Philadelphia, 1864.

Simmons, William J. *Men of Mark: Eminent, Progressive and Rising*. 1887; rpr. New York, 1968.

Smith, Daniel P. *Company K, First Alabama Regiment: or, Three Years in the Confederate Service*. N.d.; rpr. Gaithersburg, Md., 1984.

Sprague, Homer B. *History of the 13th Infantry Regiment of Connecticut Volunteers During the Great Rebellion*. Hartford, Conn., 1867.

Stanyan, John M. *A History of the Eighth Regiment of New Hampshire Volunteers: Including Its Service as Infantry, Second N.H. Cavalry, and Veteran Battalion*. Concord, N.H., 1892.

Stevens, William B. *History of the Fiftieth Regiment of Infantry, Massachusetts Volunteer Militia, in the Late War of the Rebellion*. Boston, 1907.

Strother, David Hunter. *A Virginia Yankee in the Civil War: The Diaries of David Hunter Strother*. Edited by Cecil D. Eby. Chapel Hill, 1961.

Taylor, Joe Gray. *Louisiana Reconstructed, 1863–1877*. Baton Rouge, 1974.

———. *Negro Slavery in Louisiana*. 1963; rpr. New York, 1969.

Vandal, Gilles. *Anatomy of a Tragedy: The New Orleans Riot of 1866*. Lafayette, La., 1986.

Vincent, Charles. *Black Legislators in Louisiana During Reconstruction*. Baton Rouge, 1976.

Warner, Ezra J. *Generals in Blue: Lives of the Union Commanders*. Baton Rouge, 1964.

Westwood, Howard C. *Black Troops, White Commanders, and Freedmen During the Civil War*. Carbondale, Ill., 1992.

Williams, George W. *A History of the Negro Troops in the War of the Rebellion, 1861–1865*. New York, 1888.

Williamson, Joel. *The Crucible of Race: Black-White Relations in the American South Since Emancipation*. New York, 1984.

Wilson, Joseph T. *The Black Phalanx: A History of the Negro Soldiers in the Wars of 1775, 1812, 1861–65*. 1888; rpr. New York, 1968.

Winters, John D. *The Civil War in Louisiana*. Baton Rouge, 1963.

INDEX

African Methodist Episcopal Church, 28
Alexandria, La., 49, 90–91, 95
Alfred, John A., 88n, 114n
Algiers, La., 39, 40
Anderson, William, 24
Andrew, John, 88n, 95
Andrews, George L., 51n, 78n, 81, 84–86, 90
Arkansas regiments: 17th Mounted Infantry, 71
Atchafalaya Basin, 49
Auguston, Joseph, 114n

Bailey, Joseph, 91
Banks, Nathaniel P.: assessment of black soldiers, 62, 96; forms "Forlorn Hope," 61; invests Port Hudson, 49; opinion of black officers, 45; persuades black officers to resign, 43–44; and Port Hudson campaign, 48–49, 51–52, 59–60; pulls black troops out of rural parishes, 39; purges black officers, 72–74; recruits more black soldiers, 68, 70; and Red River campaign, 90–93; replaced as department commander, 100; replaces Butler, 38; and surgeons for black troops, 98; mentioned, 37, 39, 48, 57, 75, 77, 78, 83, 85, 97, 103
Barrett, Richard, 50n
Barrett, William B., 18n, 74, 105, 109n
Bassett, Chauncey, 24, 51, 56
Baton Rouge, La., 3, 14, 29, 41, 42, 44, 45, 48, 79

Bayou Des Allemands, 113
Bayou Lafourche, 32–33, 36, 39, 41
Bayou Sera, 51
Bayou Teche, 49
Belley, William, 75
Bellville Iron Works, 40
Bertonneau, Arnold, 3, 4n, 73, 94–96, 105, 107–109, 114
Bertonneau, Julia Lacaste, 114
Berwick Bay, 32, 34, 36
Bienville Street Cemetery, 69
Big Sandy Creek, 51
"Black Brigade," 17n
Black soldiers: arms and equipment of, 45–46; distinguished from "good troops," 96n; enlistment of, 15; and the right to vote, 82, 104; families of, 30–31; illness among, 97; in state militia, 3; increased recruitment of, after Port Hudson, 66–68, 70; murdered near Jackson, La., 70; and "Star Cars," 31–32; unequal pay for, 87; Union troops' reaction to, 29, 42–43; used as common laborers, 96–97; white opposition to, 21–22, 30–31
Blake, Orwell, 114n
Bourgeau, Alfred, 77
Boutte Station, 33, 36
Breckinridge, John C., 14
Brown, Brazile, Jr., 24
Brown, John, 13
Brown, John Mifflin, 28
Burchmore, F., 81n

Bureau of Colored Troops, 96

Butler, Benjamin F.: asks Washington for reinforcements, 14; characterizes free men of color, 6; and enlistment of black soldiers, 15–16, 18; occupies New Orleans, 12; opinion of black soldiers, 13, 18–19; orders Native Guards to Bayou Lafourche, 32; and Phelps controversy, 12–14; policy on fugitive slaves, 13; praises black troops, 18; prejudices against black troops, 13, 19; reacts to Banks's purging of black officers, 82; reorganizes Native Guards, 16; replaced by Nathaniel P. Banks, 38; strategy to increase enlistment of black troops, 20–21; mentioned, 17, 23–31, 33, 72, 76, 95, 102, 105, 110

Callioux, Andre, 27, 54, 55, 57, 59, 69, 112
Camp Moore, 9
Camp Parapet, 13, 27, 89n, 102
Camp Stevens, 50n
Camp Strong, 23, 24, 28–31
Canby, Edward R. S., 100
Carter, Edward, 77n
Carter, H., 32n
Chadwick, John C., 87
Chapin, Edward P., 50
Chase, Salmon P., 16, 18
Chevalier, Pierre, 114n
Clovese, Joseph, 115n
Cobb, Howell, 65
Congo, August, 24
Congo, Wimba, 24
Connecticut regiments: 9th Infantry, 51n; 12th Infantry, 12, 19; 13th Infantry, 61, 92
"Contrabands," 13, 18, 20, 99
Corps d'Afrique: at Port Hudson, 84; becomes United States Colored Troops, 96; organization of, 70; purge of black officers from, 72–73; quality of white officers in, 79–82; and Red River campaign, 90–93; unequal pay for, 87; mentioned, 71, 74, 77, 85, 86, 89, 94

Corps d'Afrique regiments: 1st Infantry, 70, 72, 76–79, 82, 85, 90, 93; 2nd Infantry, 70, 72, 74–76, 78, 80, 82, 93; 3rd Infantry, 70, 72, 78, 81, 90, 93; 20th Infantry, 77. See also Native Guard regiments; United States Colored Troops (USCT)
Couvent, Mme. Bernard, 2
Couvent School for Orphans, 2, 17n
Crowder, John H., 28, 46, 57, 77n, 89n

Daniels, Nathan W., 25, 46, 63, 80
David, John J., 113
Davis, Edgar, 18, 41, 77n, 109n
Davis, Jennie, 80
De Forest, John William, 19
De Pass, John, 76
"Defenders of the Native Land," 1, 3, 4, 25, 107
De Gruy, Joseph, 37, 38
Delany, Martin R., 110n
Denison, George S., 16, 18
Detiége, Emile, 24, 27, 37, 38, 77n, 78, 82, 105, 109n
Devereux, John G., 7n
Dibble, Henry C., 110
Dickey, William H., 90–92
Dillard University, 109n
Donaldsonville, La., 33
Douglass, Frederick, 95
Dumas, Francis E., 19, 26–27, 47n, 74, 110, 111, 114
Dunn, Oscar, 111
Dwight, William, 52–53, 55–56, 62, 84n

East Pascagoula, Miss., 46–47
Economy Hall, 94
Emory, William H., 74, 91
English Turn, 40
Equal Rights League, 104–105, 107–108

Farragut, David G., 8–10, 26, 48, 112*n*
Fernandez, Louis, 58*n*
Finnegass, Henry, 51, 56, 81
Fisher, Belle, 80
Fitts, James, 40
Flemming, P., 76*n*
Follin, Joseph, 27, 78
"Forlorn Hope," 61
Forstall, Leon G., 44*n*
Fort Adams, 114
Fort Blakely, 101
Fort Jackson, 9–10
Fort Massachusetts, 100
Fort McComb, 40, 41, 99, 113
Fort Pike, 73, 75, 99
Fort St. Leon, 40
Fort St. Philip, 9–10
Fort Wagner, 66*n*
Foster, Charles W., 96
Foster's Creek, 51*n*
François, Louis, 108
Free men of color: description of, 4; identification with whites, 5–6; Butler's recruitment of, 17, 20; in Louisiana militia, 3; support for Confederacy, 2
Frick, Joseph, 24
Friends of Universal Suffrage, 104
Fugitive slaves: Lincoln's policy on, 13; and Militia Act, 87*n*; Phelps seeks to arm, 13; protected by Native Guards, 31*n*. *See also* "Contrabands"

Gage, John J., 113
Galpin's Restaurant, 89
Gardner, Brazil, 114
Gardner, Franklin K., 60, 61
Gardner, Samuel L., 100
Garland, J. P., 50
Garrison, William Lloyd, 95
General Banks, 46
Gibbons, Charles W., 3, 107
Gihon, John H., 80
Gla, Jacques A., 109*n*

Globe ball-room, 89
Gollis, Louis, 4*n*
Gonzales, Florville, 4*n*
Grand Army of the Republic, 112–13
Grand Ecore, 90, 91
Grant, Ulysses, 49
Griffith, John, 71
Grosvenor, William M., 75, 80–81
Grover, Cuvier, 42

Hahn, Michael, 95
Halleck, Henry W., 21
Harvard University, 85*n*
Hayes, Solomon, 75
Hickok's Hotel, 89
Hippolyte, François, 113
Hollinger, John H., 115
Horn Island, Miss., 46
Howard University, 28
Hunter, David, 13, 17*n*

Ingraham, James H., 33, 78, 105, 108, 109
Irwin, Richard B., 44
Isabelle, Robert H., 74, 105, 109*n*, 113

Jackson, Andrew, 3
Jackson, La., 70
Jackson, Miss., 102
Jackson, Stonewall, 39*n*
John P. Jackson, 46

Kansas regiments: 1st Regiment of Colored Volunteers, 17, 47*n*

Labadieville, La., 33
Lafayette, La., 49
Lake Borgne, 39
Lake Pontchartrain, 39, 41
Lane, Jim, 17
Lanusse, Armand, 2*n*, 4*n*
Larriere, Louis D., 114*n*
Lavigne, Joseph, 4*n*
Lavigne, Victor, 77*n*

Laville, Louis, 58*n*

Lawrence, Samuel, 25*n*

Levan, Louis, 114

Lewis, Alcide, 77*n*, 79

Lewis, James, 78*n*, 108*n*, 110*n*, 113*n*

Lewis, John L., 7, 9–10, 17

Lincoln, Abraham, 13, 17, 38, 66, 71, 94, 95

Logan, John L., 71

Louisiana Race Track, 23

Louisiana regiments

—Confederate: 9th Cavalry Battalion, 53; Scott's Cavalry, 71

—Union: 1st Cavalry, 50*n*, 53; 1st Engineers, 66*n*; 2nd Infantry, 62, 72

Lovell, Mansfield, 7*n*, 9–10

Maine regiments: 13th Infantry, 43; 14th Infantry, 61; 21st Infantry, 62, 72

Mallett, Jules, 77*n*

Mansfield, La., 90

Mansura, La., 92

Marsh, Mrs., 49

Martin, Theodule, 76

Massachusetts regiments: 2nd Infantry, 84, 85; 4th Artillery, 32; 6th Artillery, 53; 30th Infantry, 25; 42nd Infantry, 51, 69; 49th Infantry, 45, 64; 53rd Infantry, 97; 54th Infantry, 17*n*, 66*n*

Mechanics Institute, 106

Merriam, Henry C., 101

Michigan regiments: 6th Infantry, 61

Mississippi regiments: 39th Infantry, 53, 59

Mobile, Ala., 3, 99–102

Monroe, John T., 9–10

Montieu, Joseph L., 77*n*

Moore, Thomas O., 2, 8

Morganza, La., 94, 100

Morphy, Ernest, 74, 105, 109*n*

Morris, Morris W., 77*n*

Moss, Ehurd, 49, 78*n*

Mouton, Alfred, 33, 34

Native Guards: arrive at Baton Rouge, 41; assault at Port Hudson, 53–57; attempt to ride segregated streetcars, 31–32; black officers in, 25–28; casualties of, on May 27, pp. 57–58; composition of, 18, 36–37; Confederate assessment of, 65; criminal behavior of, 32, 36–37; and East Pascagoula raid, 46–47; importance of, in May 27 assault, 66; mustered into Union army, 17, 21; ordered to Bayou Lafourche, 32; organized as part of Louisiana militia, 2; put on alert as Farragut approaches New Orleans, 8; role in evacuation of New Orleans, 9–11; success of exaggerated by northern press, 64; support for Confederacy wanes, 7; Union troops' reaction to, 29, 42–43; veterans of, 103, 115; white opposition to, 21–22

Native Guard regiments: 1st Regiment, 17, 18, 21, 24, 26, 27, 32–35, 36, 39, 40, 45, 49, 51, 60, 70, 102, 105, 106, 108, 113; 2nd Regiment, 21, 24–26, 36, 37, 39, 46–47, 69, 70, 102, 109, 110; 3rd Regiment, 21, 25, 29, 36, 41–43, 45, 49, 51, 60, 70, 102, 112, 115; 4th Regiment, 66*n*. *See also* Corps d'Afrique regiments; United States Colored Troops (USCT)

Nelson, John A., 25, 42, 51, 53, 55–56, 63, 78, 81

New Orleans, Opelousas, and Great Western Railroad, 32, 36

New Orleans Riot of 1866, p. 106

New York regiments: 70th Infantry, 52; 114th Infantry, 39, 40; 133rd Infantry, 42

Noble, Jordan, 3*n*

Ogden, Henry D., 2, 16

Oliver, Joseph C., 78, 108*n*

Orillion, Oscar, 71

Paine, Albert E., 52*n*

Paine, Charles J., 29, 62, 72

Palmer, John, 112

Parker, Joseph G., 44*n*

Parker House, 95

Pascagoula, Miss., 46–47

Pass Rigolets, 39

Peabody, William S., 25*n*

Pensacola, Fla., 3, 101

Perkins, G. A., 80

Perkins, Hiram E., 79*n*

Phelps, John W., 12–14, 15, 17*n*, 27, 102

Phillips, Wendell, 95

Pierce, Philip, 114*n*

Pile, William A., 101–102

Pinchback, P. B. S., 24, 28, 73, 75, 82, 108, 109*n*, 111, 114

Planciancois, Anselmas, 54, 112

Pleasant Hill, 90–91

Port Hudson, 48, 51–61, 64–71, 76, 79, 81, 84–85, 87–90, 93, 95–97, 99, 105, 112, 116

Prescott, Thomas C., 58

Prouty, Elijah K., 80

"Quaker Oath," 88*n*

Quincy, Samuel M., 85–87, 89–90, 99, 116

Quinn, Captain, 55*n*

Rapp, Eugene, 18, 77*n*

Rey, Henry Louis, 6, 10*n*, 17

Rey, Octave, 18, 74, 110*n*

Ringgold, Samuel W., 74, 109*n*

Roudanez, Jean Baptiste, 94–95

St. Charles Hotel, 80

St. Cryr, Eduard, 24

St. Francisville, La., 51

St. John the Baptist Parish, 37

St. Louis, Hyppolite, 77*n*

Sauve, Celicout, 114*n*

Sauvenet, Charles, 15, 16*n*, 18, 46, 76, 78, 110

Selma, Ala., 102

Sentmanat, Charles, 77

Seream, Propher, 115

Shattuck, James W., 71

Shelby, W. B., 54*n*, 59, 61

Sheridan, Philip, 108

Ship Island, 39, 46, 70, 73, 79, 80, 85, 93, 98–100

Sidney, John, 106

Silvester, Pierre, 24

Simmesport, La., 92

Snaer, Louis A., 78, 82

Société Catholique pour l'Instruction des Ophelins dans l'Indigence, 2*n*

Southern University, 115

Spanish Fort, 101

Stafford, Spencer H., 17, 21, 24–25, 32, 39–41, 50–51, 63, 76, 79–80

Stanton, Edwin M., 13, 15, 16, 44, 45*n*, 98

"Star cars," 31–32

Stone, Charles P., 96*n*

Straight University, 109*n*

Sumner, Charles, 95

Taylor, Richard, 90, 91

Telegraph Road, 51, 53, 58, 59

Thibaut, Louis A., 77*n*

Thibodaux, La., 33

Thomas, Lorenzo, 66, 68

Thomas, Stephen, 32–35

Touro Building, 20, 23, 31

Trask, Frank L., 75, 79

Twiggs, David E., 7*n*

Ullmann, Daniel, 66, 70, 74, 79, 98, 100

United States Colored Troops (USCT): 4th Cavalry, 97; 73rd Infantry, 96, 99–102; 74th Infantry, 96, 98, 99, 103*n*; 75th Infantry, 96, 100, 103*n*; 91st Infantry, 99; 92nd Infantry, 100; 96th Infantry, 103; 104th Infantry, 110*n*. *See also* Corps d'Afrique regiments; Native Guard regiments

Vermillionville, La., 49
Vermont regiments: 8th Infantry, 25*n*, 32–35, 79*n*
Vicksburg, Miss., 48, 61, 102
Villeverde, Joseph, 75

Warmoth, Henry Clay, 111
Weitzel, Godfrey, 32–35, 38
Wilson, Henry, 79, 98
Wilson, Joseph T., 18